HOW TO PLAY
THE
UKULELE

HOW TO PLAY
THE
UKULELE

The ultimate step-by-step guide

Terry Burrows

SIRIUS

Author's Acknowledgements

The author would like to thank Louis Burrows for his photographic work on the project; Adam Ironside (D'Addario UK) and Max Nye (Fender Musical Instruments Corporation) for providing materials for the photoshoot; Vanessa Daubney and Peter Ridley of Arcturus Publishing for getting the project off the ground.

Images

With the exception of the images listed under the Picture Credits, all original photography is by Louis Burrows and Terry Burrows.

Picture Credits

Getty Images: /John Springer Collection/CORBIS, 6; /Haeckel Collection/ ullstein bild, 7; /Andrew Lepley/Redferns, 10 (left); /Hulton Archive, 10 (right); /Michael Ochs Archives, 11.

Public Domain: 8 (both), 9.

SIRIUS

This edition published in 2018 by Sirius Publishing, a division of
Arcturus Publishing Limited,
26/27 Bickels Yard, 151–153 Bermondsey Street,
London SE1 3HA

ISBN: 978-1-78888-330-6
AD006308UK

Printed in China

Contents

A Bit of Background

The ukulele is a surprisingly young instrument, only emerging in the Pacific island of Hawaii during the 1880s. Yet its lineage can be traced back to the first stringed musical instruments, namely the musical bow, which we know from ancient cave paintings have existed for more than 15,000 years.

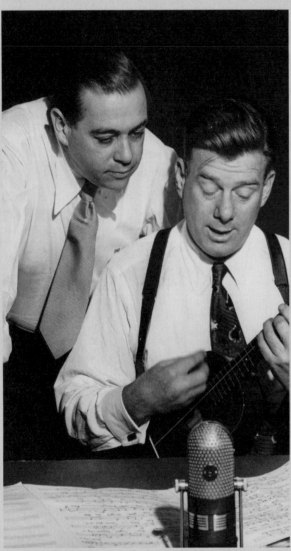

Arthur Godfrey (right), a key figure in the popularity of the ukulele.

HOW DO YOU SAY THAT?

Since the instrument first became popular in the United States during the 1920s, the generally accepted pronunciation has been "Yoo-Ker-Lay-Lee". In fact it's a Hawaiian word that sounds closer to "Ooo-Koo-Lay-Lay"; singer and broadcaster Arthur Godfrey attempted to correct this mispronunciation on his 1950 signature song 'Makin' Love Ukulele Style'. In spite of his best efforts it failed to catch on.

How it Works

All stringed instruments could be said to hail from the musical bow, which itself is likely to have evolved from the humble hunting bow. Created by tightly stretching a string made from animal intestines between the ends of a branch, plucking the string produced an audible sound; stretching the tension of the strings or holding them down at different positions along the bow would produce sounds of different pitches. And this is the fundamental principle behind every modern-day stringed instrument – the guitar, lute, cello, violin, double bass… and the ukulele.

Islanders in Hawaiian national dress photographed in around 1890 – barely a decade after the instrument first emerged.

The underlying physics also relates to all acoustic musical instruments. When a string is plucked, the vibrations cause movement in the molecules between the string and our ears. Indeed, this is how we perceive ALL sound.

A tightened string on its own, however, doesn't create much of a disturbance and so will not be very loud. In order to make the moving string displace more molecules it needs to be in contact with some kind of soundboard – a larger object that also vibrates when the string is plucked. On a ukulele and other similar instruments – such as the guitar, violin or cello – one end of the string is always in contact with a bridge saddle that sits on top of the body, which is effectively a large, hollow wooden box. This means that when the string is played, the vibrations pass through the saddle causing the body itself to resonate. This creates more energy through the greater disturbance of molecules, resulting in a louder volume.

Origins of the Ukulele

The ukulele is part of the guitar family. Emerging during the Renaissance from stringed instruments such as the Arabic oud and European lute and vihuela, by the end of the 18th century the guitar had evolved to its modern form, with six strings, the characteristic "figure-of-eight" body and a set of fixed frets on the fingerboard, positioned mathematically to produce chromatic intervals of a semitone (or half-step).

As the guitar proliferated throughout Europe, regional variations began to appear. One of these, hailing from the Portuguese island of Madeira, was a miniature four-string model called a machete ("ma-shet"). Popular among sailors on long voyages, in 1879 three Madeiran cabinet makers – Manuel Nunes, José do Espírito Santo, and Augusto Dias – arrived in Hawaii on board the *SS Ravenscrag*, and, according to reports in the local newspaper began "delighting the people with nightly street concerts".

King Kalakaua of Hawaii (1836–91), the first patron of the ukulele.

ROY SMECK (1900-1994)

Billed as "The Wizard of the Strings", Roy Smeck was accomplished on the guitar, banjo and ukulele. One of the first musical stars of the radio in the United States, Smeck was hugely important in popularising the ukulele in the 1920s, developing an assortment of eye-catching novelty styles, including playing the ukulele behind his back and with his teeth. Film exists of him performing Rubinstein's 'Melody in F' on a soprano ukulele: among the formidable playing skills on display, during one passage he breaks into some high-speed finger-tapping, a technique where the sound is created by the left hand "hammering" runs of notes down against the fingerboard. Eddie Van Halen would popularise this style of playing on the electric guitar more than half a century later.

The ukulele quickly became popular on Hawaii and swiftly evolved in its own way, with construction from local koa wood rather than the pine used in Madeira, as well as a new style of tuning. It also developed a new name, ukulele, which literally translates as "jumping flea". (Nobody knows for sure where this came from, although one explanation is that the player's hand strums so quickly that it moves like a jumping flea.) Fundamental, though, to the popularity of the ukulele on the island was the patronage of the Hawaiian Royal Family, in particular King Kalakaua, an enthusiastic musician who had already provided the lyrics to 'Hawai'i Pono'i', which is now the official state song of the island. Kalakaua would often perform for visitors at official gatherings, accompanied by his own musical group, The Singing Boys. By the time the island was annexed by the United States in 1898, the ukulele had become Hawaii's national instrument.

Beyond the Island

It was the 1915 Panama-Pacific International Exposition that first brought the ukulele to mainland America. A world's fair held over ten months in San Francisco, California, the Hawaiian Pavilion exhibit gave many Americans an introduction to the island's culture, the music of the ukulele and the lap steel guitar (Hawaii's other significant musical export). Popular Hawaiian-themed songs began to emerge, and the instrument was taken up by stars of vaudeville and early radio, such as Roy Smeck and Cliff Edwards.

The ukulele quickly became one of the most popular instruments of the 1920s: it was cheap to buy, easy to learn, portable, and there was plenty of sheet music available. During this time, ukulele makers also began to experiment with instruments of different sizes and ranges of notes: in addition to the original soprano ukulele, larger "concert"

and "tenor" models began to appear. Although other types of ukulele – both larger and smaller – have since been established, these original three sizes remain the most commonly played.

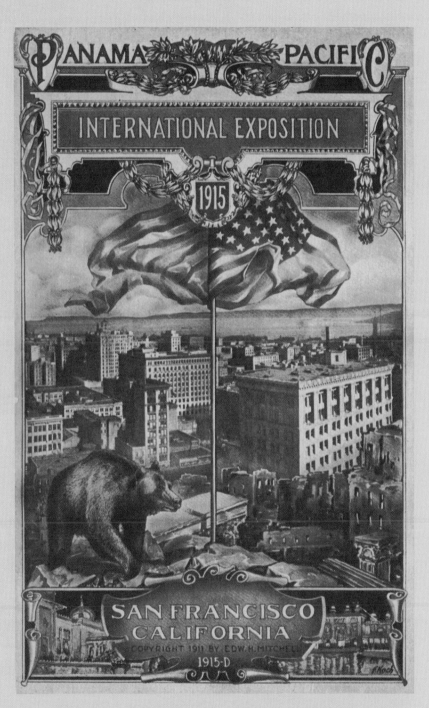

The Panama-Pacific International Exhibition introduced both the ukulele and Hawaiian music to the United States in 1915.

A Global Instrument

Across the Atlantic, a home-grown celebrity emerged during the late 1920s. George Formby (1904–61) was widely responsible for the popularity of the ukulele in the United Kingdom. A star of music hall, feature films and gramophone records, Formby's fame was such that even now, more than half a century after his death, many of the songs he popularized – 'When I'm Cleaning Windows' and 'With My Little Stick of Blackpool Rock' to name but two – remain at the core of the modern ukulele repertoire… even if they were usually performed on a banjo ukulele. By the 1950s, the music of George Formby and Tessie O'Shea – another ukulele star of that era – had fallen from fashion in the UK and interest in the instrument waned.

The Second Coming

By the end of the 1930s, even though the vogue for Hawaiian music in the United States had dwindled, its

Jake Shimabukuro, a modern master of the ukulele.

THE BANJO UKULELE

George Formby's instrument of choice, the "banjolele" combines the neck and scale of a soprano ukulele with the body of a banjo. The bridge saddle is mounted on calf skin tightened around a circular frame of wood or metal. It gives the instrument the tone and greater volume of the banjo but with the ease of playability of the uke.

influence continued to be heard when the lap steel became the first type of guitar to be "electrified". It wasn't be until the end of the 1940s and the early days of television that the uke enjoyed its second wave of popularity, cultivated mainly by American presenter Arthur Godfrey (1903–83). On his national television show, the "Ole Redhead", as he billed himself, was a passionate advocate of the ukulele, even providing his viewers with weekly lessons. One of the first successful on-air commercial sales celebrities, Godfrey convinced the noted instrument manufacturer Mario Maccaferri to produce a playable plastic ukulele that he would plug on his show. First produced in 1949, the Maccaferri Islander range sold for just $5.95. They remained in production for almost two decades; although they were hardly the finest instruments, around nine million plastic ukuleles were sold during that time.

Although the ukulele went out of fashion in the 1960s, that era did produce perhaps the most famous song ever to be connected with the instrument. In 1968, at the peak of the hippie era, singer Tiny Tim – who had learnt to play using one of Maccaferri's plastic ukes – enjoyed a global hit with a song from the 1920s, 'Tiptoe Through the Tulips'.

The Third Wave

Towards the end of the 20th century the ukulele enjoyed a huge resurgence in popularity, which has continued ever since. New artists emerged, new manufacturers began building high-quality instruments and viral videos on the internet all served to promote interest in the ukulele. In 1993 Hawaii's most celebrated musician Israel Kamakawiwo'ole recorded a ukulele medley of 'Over the Rainbow' and 'What a Wonderful World'. It was not until two years after his death in 1997 that the song began to make regular appearances in TV shows and movies, eventually selling millions of copies.

More recently, Honolulu-born Jake Shimabukuro (b.1976) became a worldwide internet sensation after posting videos of solo performances. To many he now represents the state-of-the-art as far as virtuoso ukulele playing is concerned.

Herbert Khaury (1932–96), known professionally as Tiny Tim, was not only a cult musical celebrity but an important archivist of songs from earlier in the 20th century.

The Basics

The ukulele is all about having fun. As a musical instrument it's never been taken too seriously, and is sometimes viewed as little more than a toy: after all, it's small, it's not very loud and it's very easy to learn. And even if you become a virtuoso on the uke (and there are some amazing players out there), it's unlikely to be your ticket to fame and fortune. But it's a great instrument, especially if you want to accompany your own voice… and it doesn't call for a huge investment of time to get up and running.

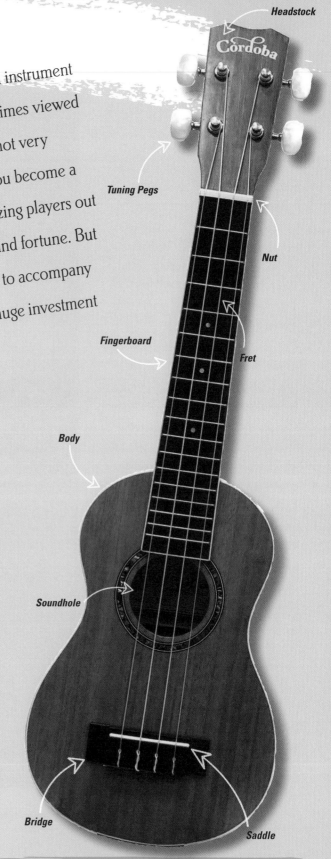

Headstock

Tuning Pegs

Nut

Fingerboard

Fret

Body

Soundhole

Bridge

Saddle

The Components

Let's kick things off with a look at the individual parts that make up the ukulele. Here is a soprano model, sometimes known as a "standard" ukulele. (You'll soon discover that there are other types of uke – some larger, some smaller – but they all comprise the same basic components. Although there have been instruments made from other materials the ukulele is traditionally built using different types of wood. The body and the neck are built separately and then fixed together using a strong glue.

The first instruments to arrive on Hawaii were built from pine. This quickly changed in favour of locally grown koa; with its attractive dark grain, koa is endemic to the islands and was traditionally used to build canoes. Many of the highest quality ukuleles still use bodies built from koa, but since it's now in limited supply and expensive, other hardwoods such as mahogany are more often used instead. Since the upper surface of the body is largely responsible for its tone, other woods, such as cedar, spruce and redwood are often used for the top of the soundbox. Cheaper ukuleles tend to be made from plywood or laminates; they will still "work" but they won't sound quite as nice.

The neck is usually cut from a single piece of mahogany with a thin strip of rosewood or ebony glued on the top – this is the fretboard, which accommodates the nickel wire frets.

Bridge and Saddle

The strings are fitted at the bridge, which is fixed to the top of the soundbox and sets the correct spacing between each string. Depending on the type of bridge you have on your instrument, the strings either slot into the back or pass through a channel where they are knotted and held in place. The strings then pass over the saddle which regulates their height above the fingerboard – this is known as the "action". The saddles found on cheaper instruments are usually made from molded plastic, but carved bone is more common on better-quality models.

Nut

At the opposite end of the neck, the string passes through the nut – again, usually cut from bone or plastic – which sets the spacing and height at that position. If the nut has not been correctly set, the strings at that end of the instrument may buzz against the frets.

Tuning Pegs

The strings finally slot into the tuning pegs; these tighten or slacken the tension of the string – and that is how we tune the ukulele. On most modern instruments, the tuning pegs feature a gear wheel connected to the pin that holds the string in place and allows for a very fine degree of tuning (see right). Tuning pegs are sometimes also known as tuners or machine heads.

Bridge and saddle

Bone nut

Geared tuning peg

Different Strokes...

There are plenty of methods you can use to learn the ukulele; and this book will offer you several alternatives.

You can achieve some useful basics simply by looking at the overhead chord charts that we feature throughout the book. Each one provides you with its correct name as well as the notes that make up that chord. If you prefer, though, you could just ignore all that and study a handful of shapes that sound nice when played together. With half-a-dozen well chosen chords you can strum along to versions of many of the most popular songs ever written.

You could even just look at the photographs in the Chord Dictionary (pages 76-101) and simply copy where each of the fingers is supposed to go.

We also offer the possibility of backing up your playing with some solid music theory, as well as "proper" written music, be it standard notation – the "dots" on the five lines – or the more easily interpreted tablature (TAB).

Whichever path you choose, though, within 30 minutes of picking up a uke for the first time, you should be able to get something musical out of it. We're not kidding!

Let's start with a look at those overhead diagrams. The main teaching element we use throughout the book depicts the

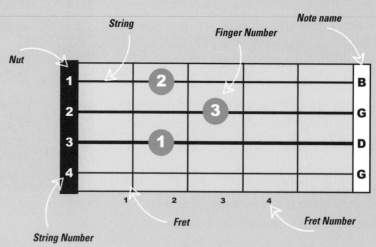

The chord diagram illustrates the finger number and fret to be played on each string, along with the names of each note.

fingerboard shown from above. This is mainly how we illustrate chord shapes – although it's also handy for showing how best to play scales. Let's look at each element one step at a time.

The Nut is the small piece of bone or plastic positioned at the top of the fingerboard. It has four grooves that act as spacers for each of the strings. On the chord diagram it's represented as the black block on the left, along with the string numbers.

The Strings are numbered from "1" to "4" – although perhaps counterintuitively, the "top string" ("1") represents the one closest to the floor when you're holding the instrument. (You can actually see this from the thickness of the strings on the diagram.)

The Frets are represented by the vertical lines that cross the fretboard. They are numbered beneath the diagram.

The Finger Numbers are indicated by the red circles on the fretboard. These tell you which fingers you need to use to hold each string against the fret.
"1" represents the 1st/index finger
"2" indicates the 2nd/middle finger
"3" is the 3rd/ring finger
"4" is the 4th/little finger (or "pinky").

In the example shown here – for a G major chord – the 1st finger is held down at the 2nd fret of the 3rd string; the 2nd finger plays the 2nd fret of the 1st string and the 3rd finger plays the 3rd fret of the 2nd string; the 4th string is played "open" or unfretted.

CHORDS IN PRINTED MUSIC

In printed sheet music for the ukulele you might sometimes come across chord shapes above the notes of the melody line. These tell you HOW to play the chords and WHEN to play them. They are similar to our own more detailed chord charts only rotated at 90 degrees. The four vertical lines are the strings; the horizontal lines are the frets; the black dots the finger positions, and the circle above the nut is an instruction to play an open string.

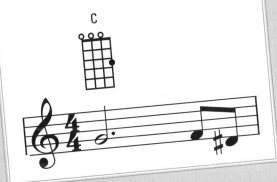

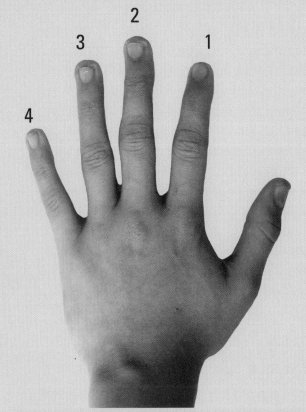

When playing notes with the left hand, or picking strings with the right hand, the fingers are numbered from "1" to "4"; where the thumb is used for picking it is denoted by "T".

The Note Names are shown alongside each string on the right of the diagram. So the notes that make up that G major chord are, from top to bottom, B, G, D and G.

The Photograph of the chord being played, taken from the front of the fingerboard, provides you with an extra check. (To make the hand positions clearer we've used a tenor ukulele for all the fingerboard photography throughout the book.)

The overhead chord diagrams are reinforced with photographs that show the correct positioning of each finger.

Tablature

Alongside some of the chord charts – notably those in the Chord Dictionary (see pages 76–101) – you'll see three columns of numbers. This is tablature or "TAB". It's similar to the system in common use among guitar players. It's easy to follow as it simply tells you which frets have to be held down on which string. The first column gives you the TAB for the G major chord shown in the diagram – so the 1st, 2nd and 3rd strings play the 2nd, 3rd, and 2nd frets respectively. The second and third tablature columns provide two alternative versions of the same the same chord but using different shapes at different positions on the fingerboard. TAB is also used throughout as an accompaniment to standard music notation, usually provided the notes of a melody on a separate line underneath.

Naming the Notes

Okay, we're not going to teach you *all* of the intricacies of reading music in a book like this, but some of you are certain to have had music lessons, so we've also included

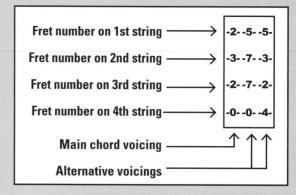

Tablature provides a graphical illustration of the ukulele fingerboard when viewed from above.

some standard notation. (And in truth, there's no better way of showing how a melody should be played.) So let's start with a VERY basic lesson for you. Music teachers look away now!

Let's begin with the notes. All music is made up of twelve different notes. These are probably best viewed as the notes of a piano keyboard as shown on the diagram below. Notes increase in pitch (they get higher) as you move from left to right along the keyboard. The white notes on the keyboard are named from A to G. To complicate matters, each of the black notes can have two possible names relating to the white notes either side. These are called "enharmonic" notes and each type has its own name and symbol: the sharp (♯) and the flat (♭).

If you look at the way the notes are named you will see that these sequences repeat, so when you get to G, the next white note along the keyboard is once again called A. Although it has the same name, it is one octave higher in pitch than the previous note of the same name.

AMERICAN TERMINOLOGY

There are a small number of musical terms where the United States differs from Europe and the rest of the world. We'll generally be using European terminology here, although we'll reference both where necessary. Here is a quick conversion table:

EUROPE	UNITED STATES
Semibreve	Whole Note
Minim	Half Note
Crotchet	Quarter Note
Quaver	Eighth Note
Semiquaver	Sixteenth Note
Tone	Step (Whole Step)
Semitone	Half Step

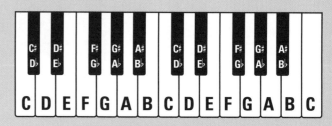

Two octaves of notes named on a piano keyboard.

Intervals

The interval between any two adjacent notes is called a semitone (or a half step in the US). This represents one-twelfth of an octave. Looking at the white keys, B and C are one semitone apart, as are E and F. However, the other white keys are two semitones. This interval is called a tone (or a step in the US).

Music is written on a five-line grid called a staff. Symbols can be positioned on and between the lines of the staff to indicate the pitch and duration of a single note to be played. Notes that are predominantly on the upper end of the piano – the range used in most melodies – are positioned on a "treble" staff, which is prefixed by a treble clef symbol (𝄞). The clef defines the notes on and between each line on the staff. For a treble clef, the notes on the lines are fixed as E, G, B, D and F. The notes between the lines are F, A, C and E. (Notes can also be extended above and below the staff when needed – like the first two notes shown on the line of music below.)

We can see how the white notes are shown on the staff, but what about the enharmonic black notes? These appear on the line or space after which they are named and are shown with either the flat or sharp symbol to the left of the head of the note.

If you look at the lines of music below you can see that each of these notes is represented by a circular symbol. These symbols will change in accordance with the length of the note, although it is the position of the circle (the notehead) on the staff that will always define the pitch of the note. More of that later, though.

Okay, that should be enough to keep you going for now. Let's get ready to make some noise.

UKE FOR LEFTIES

Playing left-handed ukulele is not a problem. The instrument's body is symmetrical so all you have to do is remove the strings and put them back on in reverse order, so that the "bottom" string becomes the "top" string. When working through the book, though, you'll have to make a mental adjustment when following chord diagrams or photographs and think of them as seen in a mirror.

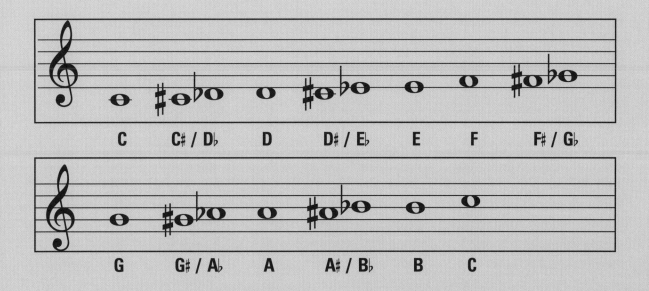

C   C♯ / D♭   D   D♯ / E♭   E   F   F♯ / G♭

G   G♯ / A♭   A   A♯ / B♭   B   C

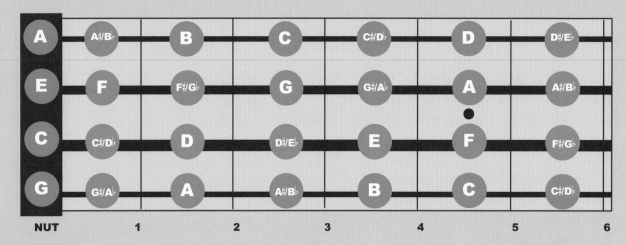

A	A#/B♭	B	C	C#/D♭	D	D#/E♭
E	F	F#/G♭	G	G#/A♭	A	A#/B♭
C	C#/D♭	D	D#/E♭	E	F	F#/G♭
G	G#/A♭	A	A#/B♭	B	C	C#/D♭

NUT **1** **2** **3** **4** **5** **6**

The Open Strings

Now let's take a detailed look at the ukulele's fingerboard. The soprano, concert and tenor ukuleles are by far the most commonly played. And, conveniently for us, in spite of their differing sizes they all use exactly the same standard open-string tuning, the notes G–C–E–A. This means that every note on every string on every fret will be the same, which ever type of instrument you have.

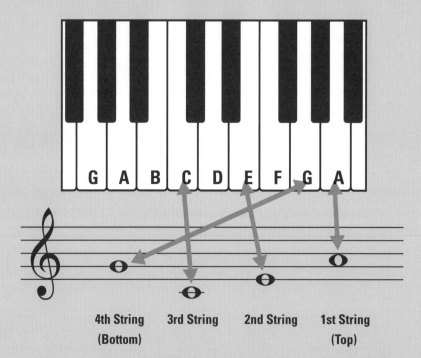

4th String **3rd String** **2nd String** **1st String**
(Bottom) **(Top)**

Standard Tuning

The ukulele has one very unusual quirk: unlike most other stringed instruments, it uses what is known as "re-entrant" tuning. This means that the open strings do not ascend or descend in order of pitch. Unlike on a guitar, the bottom string on the ukulele is *not* the lowest in pitch – that's the C on the open 3rd string. The reason behind this tuning seems to have been lost in history: one possibility is that although a low G 4th string might have been preferred, it was difficult to achieve using the catgut from which the strings were made in the late 1800s. Using modern string technology, it *is* possible to string a tenor ukulele with a low G and simply use it as if you were playing a guitar with just the top four strings – and some players prefer to do this. That said, the character of the ukulele sound is very much tied up with its unusual system of tuning.

Before the 1940s, though, it seems to have been common to tune the ukulele one tone higher (A-D-F#-B), which is sometimes now called English tuning. So if you are lucky enough to find an old pre-war songbook then you'll probably need to retune your instrument accordingly. (Some modern players do actually prefer this tuning for a "sweeter"sound.)

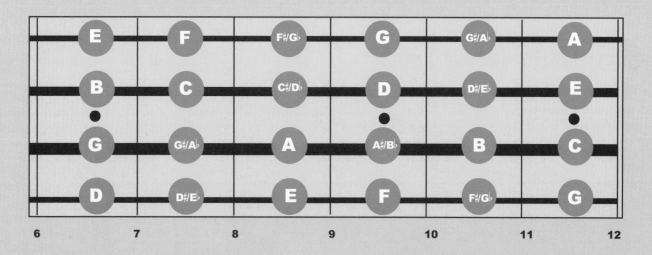

	6	7	8	9	10	11	12

Alternative Ukulele Tunings

Fifths	G–D–A–E	Pocket Ukulele	D–G–B–E
Slack	G–C–E–G	Baritone Ukulele*	D–G–B–E
English	A–D–F#–B	Bass Ukulele	E–A–D–G
Canadian	Low A–D–F#–B	*one octave lower than pocket ukulele	

There are a number of other alternative ukulele open-string tunings that are occasionally used (see above) but our focus throughout the book will be on standard tuning.

The Fingerboard

The notes on a standard-tuned ukulele fingerboard are shown on the diagram across the top of these two pages. You can see that the note name on the 12th fret of each string is the same as for the open string, although the pitch will be one octave higher. Many of the smaller ukuleles only have a dozen frets on the fingerboard, however that can sometimes extend beyond fifteen frets on larger instruments. In these cases the notes on the 13th, 14th and 15th frets would be one octave higher than notes on the 1st, 2nd and 3rd frets respectively.

It's worth taking a little time to get to know the notes on the fingerboard, especially those on the 3rd string, which, as the lowest pitched string, is often used to play the note that defines the key of a chord.

PLAY THE GUITAR?

If you can play the guitar, then learning the ukulele will be a cinch. Although the tuning of the four strings of the uke is not the same as the top four strings on the guitar, it conveniently has the same note intervals between each string. (Well, kind of, anyway... we'll ignore for now that the bottom string is, relatively speaking, an octave higher!) This means that any chord shapes you can make on the top four strings of a guitar will also work on the ukulele. For example, the same fingering for the D major chord on a guitar – the 2nd, 3rd and 2nd frets on the top three strings – creates a G major chord on the ukulele.

Getting Started

In this section we'll take a look at the different types of ukulele available and how to go about choosing one. And before we get down to the nitty-gritty of making a sound, you'll need to know how to hold your instrument correctly and, above all, how to get it in tune.

Pocket ukulele

Soprano ukulele

Concert ukulele

Tenor ukulele

Choosing your Ukulele

Selecting an instrument can be a daunting prospect for a beginner. What size? How much do I spend? What shape? What do I want to do with it? Let's see if we can help out here.

There are seven recognised types of ukulele. Their differences are in physical size as well as their scale lengths – the measurement between the point where the string touches the nut and the bridge saddle. From smallest to largest they are: pocket, soprano, concert, tenor, baritone, bass and contrabass. These ukuleles have different ranges of notes. The smallest instruments play the highest-pitched sounds; by the time you get to

the baritone ukulele you will start to notice distinctly acoustic guitar-like tones.

So which one do you choose? By far the most commonly seen ukulele is the original soprano instrument, although many serious players favour the tenor as the increased scale length enables playing higher up the fingerboard.

In terms of how much you should spend, you can pay anything from below £20 to over £2000 for a ukulele. As a beginner, with care it's quite possible to get something playable at the lower end of that range and then move on to greater things if you take to the instrument. At the top end of the scale you are often paying for premium woods and fantastic craftsmanship, which a novice may struggle to appreciate. At the opposite end, though, cheap starter kits are often poorly made, sound horrible and are difficult to keep in tune. The cheapest ukes can also be cursed with poor intonation, meaning they go out of tune the further you play along the fingerboard. When you're a beginner, it simply has to be fun or you won't want to carry on, and there's no worse deterrent than a nasty instrument.

The best known ukulele brands, such as Mahalo, Kala and Luna all produce ranges of decent-quality instruments that won't break the bank. And many of the top names in the guitar world – Gretsch, Fender, Gibson, Epiphone – also produce ranges of ukes. Spending between £50 and £100 on your first instrument should see you with something quite playable.

Shifting Shapes

Nearly all ukuleles come in the classic figure-of-eight guitar shape, but over the years many makers have toyed with that format. The most common alternative body shape is the "pineapple", a design that dates back to the late 1920s and now has quite a niche following. The larger body size was developed to enable small soprano ukuleles to produce greater volume. A more recent innovation coming from the world of the electric guitar has been the cutaway ukulele, with an indentation in the body around the neck joint that allows easier access to the higher frets.

The Electric Uke

The recent rise in popularity enjoyed by the ukulele has been accompanied by an inevitable demand for instruments that can be used easily in a live environment. With it's small size and low volume, amplifying the sound of an acoustic ukulele on stage using a microphone is not an enviable prospect. This has resulted in a new type of electroacoustic ukulele that can be played acoustically but also has an inbuilt pickup

Preamp and pickup controls

Pineapple soprano model   *Kala electroacoustic tenor cutaway*

that can be connected to an amplifier or PA mixer. If you intend taking to the stage with your ukulele then these are worth a serious look.

It's also possible to "electrify" an existing acoustic ukulele. There are numerous systems that can be installed without causing any damage to the body of your instrument. The most common approach is to fit a piezo pickup to the bridge that can be removed when you want to revert to acoustic playing.

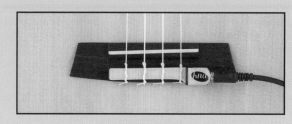

KNA Piezo Pickup

Getting into Position

Learning the ukulele is not the same as getting to grips with classical guitar, where there's basically one approved way of doing things. It's really up to you to decide how you feel most comfortable. The uke can be played standing up or sitting down. It can also be held with or without a strap. (Although mostly without.)

Three Points of Contact

Whether you're standing or sitting, the best practice is to observe the "three points" rule.

1. The back of the ukulele is held against your lower chest/upper stomach area.

2. The right forearm folds around the bottom of the body just below the bridge and gently "clamps" the ukulele in position.

3. The neck is cradled between the thumb and fingers of the left hand.

The key to holding your ukulele is balance. The instrument should be held with the neck raised at an angle of around 10-30 degrees, and with the neck held slightly away from you. Don't grip the uke for dear life! It's an informal instrument and will benefit from a relaxed, "loosey-goosey" posture. And, as it's a small resonating acoustic instrument, if you hold it too tightly against your chest your clothing will act as a dampener and you'll lose volume and brightness of the tone. Frankly, these issues tend to be minimised when you are playing in the sitting position as you'll be less likely to worry about dropping your ukulele.

For some beginners there's a tendency to hold the ukulele so that the fingerboard is almost horizontal, and this is mainly so they can see more easily what they are playing. Try to avoid this – it's counterproductive as the angle makes it even more difficult to fret notes and chords.

Strapping Up

Most ukuleles are not equipped to be worn with a strap – it's really not that traditional – but there are a growing number of converts. One clear advantage is that on stage you don't have to worry about dropping your uke, which is surprisingly easy when it's basically wedged under your arm against your chest. And while soprano and concert ukuleles are small and lightweight, tenor and baritone instruments can get fatiguing over long periods. There is a counter-argument that, with their lightweight bodies, ukuleles don't balance naturally when on a strap in the same way that a solid-body electric guitar does, so you will need to support the neck constantly to keep it in position.

It's possible to use a standard guitar strap with a ukulele, although better to buy a purpose-made strap since these are lighter, narrower and more comfortable.

Fitting Your Own Strap Buttons

If you want to play with a strap and your ukulele is not suitably equipped, don't worry – strap buttons can be fitted with a minimum of fuss. A set can be bought for a few pounds in any guitar store, and installing them is a ten-minute job. (Be warned, though, it *will* require you to drill two holes in your ukulele, so it's probably best to avoid converting that rare vintage Sam Kamaka model!

All you need for the job is some masking tape, a small drill (or rotary tool) and a cross-head screwdriver. You fit one button to the base of the body (bottom left) and the other on the neck joint (bottom right).

1. Place a small piece of masking tape over where the hole is to be drilled and mark the point with a pen. (The tape not only gives you your target but also will protect the bodywork of the ukulele.)

2. Carefully drill the hole.

3. Take the strap button, push the screw through the centre hole, and fix into the body of the ukulele using the screwdriver.

A common alternative makes use of just one strap button fitted to the base of the body – the other end of the strap is tied and knotted around the headstock. This provides a little better balance.

If you don't fancy drilling into your uke then there are plenty of alternatives you can look at, including systems that enable the strap to clip either side of the soundhole, and experiments using hook and loop-type fastening tape.

Soprano ukulele with purpose-made D'Addario strap.

Fitting strap buttons is simple but requires drilling holes in the body.

Thumb Position

As is so often the case, the best practice is not always the one that's easiest or comes most naturally. Unless you've had some classical guitar training, when you first pick up a ukulele you are likely to want to wrap the thumb of your left hand right around the back of the neck so that it hangs over the edge of the fingerboard. It's not greatly surprising that this feels like the most comfortable way holding the instrument – after all, the fingerboard is *so* narrow at the nut that it feels natural to do it that way. And there are many ukulele players who use this hand position quite happily. It isn't necessarily the best practice, though, even if it can be a good alternative technique for some situations. That said, if you try out the wrapping method (see box right) and feel more comfortable with it – don't worry, the ukulele police won't come knocking on your door. (They only do that for people who play with a pick!)

Our suggestion is that when fretting chords and notes you hold the thumb firmly against the back of neck in the "classical" manner. This will help to provide the right pressure when pushing the strings onto the frets – you're effectively clamping them between the thumb and fingers. The exact position of the thumb will depend on the size of your hands and which type of

The alternative to the classical thumb position is to wrap the thumb over the top of the fingerboard. This has the advantage of being more comfortable and also provides more natural support for the neck as it cradles between the thumb and fingers. This technique may work well for open-string chords where the thumb can be "hidden" alongside or behind the nut, but further along the fingerboard it does become easy to unintentionally mute the bottom string.

ukulele you're playing – for a soprano or concert it's fine for the thumb to be held closer to the top of the neck.

Some experienced players are quite adept at using both thumb techniques. They use the comfortable thumb-wrap when playing "open-string" chords. (These are the chords that are formed using the first two or three frets of the fingerboard and make use of at least one unfretted or "open" string.) However, when playing single-note melodies or lead parts – or chords that use an index-finger barre – they revert to the classical thumb position.

"Classical" thumb position

Striking the Notes

Stating the obvious for a moment, to make a sound you have to strike the strings of your ukulele with your right hand. The most common method is to use your 1st finger (index finger), brushing the nail *down* across all four strings from bottom to top; or dragging the pad of the finger back *up* across the strings from top to bottom. Strumming patterns are created using these combinations of downstrokes and upstrokes.

This is by no means the end of the story. More complex sounds can be produced by brushing *all* of the fingers over the strings or by integrating the thumb into strumming patterns. A different approach is to integrate the fingerpicking styles used in classical and bluegrass music, where the thumb and fingers play specific strings. You'll discover more of these as you work your way through the book.

Developing your strumming technique is absolutely fundamental to mastering the instrument. Unlike the world of the guitar, watching an expert play the ukulele you're as likely to be dazzled by the complexities of the right hand than anything happening on the fingerboard.

Most of the picking and strumming is done using the index finger.

Using a Pick

Okay, the ukulele police won't really arrest you for this! (Their sole job is to enforce the When-I'm-Cleaning-Windows Prevention Act.) Playing with a pick (or a plectrum as they are sometimes known) is perfectly acceptable. However, as with the "rules" regarding the left-hand thumb, if you play solely with a pick then you'll certainly be restricting yourself when it comes to the range of possibilities offered by the instrument.

The pick is a small triangular object with a rounded tip (see left). You hold the pick firmly between your thumb and index finger and strike the string with the tip. You can strike down from above the string or up from below; to play superfast, single-note solos you need to alternate swiftly between the two strokes.

It *is* possible to use a regular plastic or tortoiseshell guitar pick wit ha ukulele, but these tend to be quite hard and can easily damage the body if it makes contact. A much better plan is to use a special ukulele pick made from thick felt or leather.

Using a pick is effective when playing single-note melodies.

Tuning Methods

Using standard ukulele tuning, the notes, from the 4th string up to the 1st string, are G–C–E–A. It's clear that if you are playing with other musicians, your uke needs to be strictly in tune with their instruments or everything will sound terrible. When playing on your own, though, the only important concern is that the four strings of your ukulele are in tune relative to one another. So let's take a look at some different approaches to tuning.

Using Technology

In the old days, if you didn't have a piano in the house, you'd need tuning forks or pitch pipes to get in tune. Nowadays we have modern technology that "listens" to the string and tells you when it's in tune. It can be a dedicated electronic tuning device or an app on your smart phone or tablet. This is a good deal easier, not to mention more accurate, than using your ears.

D'Addario headstock tuner

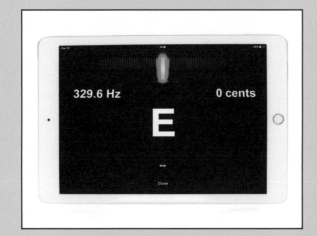

Guitar Toolkit tuning app

TUNING TO A GUITAR

If you have a guitar handy (and it's in tune) you can use the top two strings (E and B) to tune your ukulele:

Ukulele
1st string (A)
2nd string (E)
3rd string (C)
4th string (G)

Guitar
E string, 5th fret
E string, open
B string, 1st fret
E string

Headstock tuners work by sensing the vibrations of the string. To tune the 1st string you have to do little more than pick the string and turn the tuning peg button gradually until the electronic tuner indicates that you have a perfect A note. Then you do the same for the other three strings. The beauty of headstock tuners is that you can leave them fitted while you play so that you can continually check your tuning.

More traditional electronic tuners work on a visual meter, so you play the note, turn the tuning peg, and the meter will indicate when you are in tune. There are numerous smart phone or tablet apps available so there really is no excuse for not being in perfect tune.

Tuning to a Fixed Reference

This means using your ears to match the strings on your ukulele to a set of tones that you know to be definitively correct, say using a piano or electronic keyboard or one of the many sets of tuning tones you can find online. The notes for tuning with a piano keyboard are shown on page 18. The open 3rd string equates to "Middle C" on a piano, so start with this. Play the note on the piano and while it sustains play the open string while tightening or slackening the string until you hit the correct note. Continue with the 2nd, 1st and 4th strings.

Relative Tuning

If you can get the top A of your ukulele in tune using a keyboard or other reference tone then it's possible to tune the other strings from there. This was one of the oldest and most widely used methods of tuning before the advent of electronic tuners.

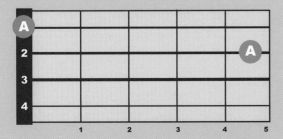

1. Using a reference source, tune the 1st string (A). Play the 5th fret of the 2nd string and adjust the pitch until it matches the open 1st string.

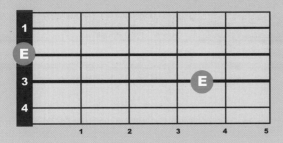

2. Play the open 2nd string. While it's still ringing, play the 4th fret of the 3rd string; adjust the pitch of the 3rd string until the two are in tune.

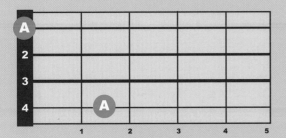

3. Play the 2nd fret of the 4th string and adjust the pitch until it matches the open 1st string. Your ukulele should now be in perfect tune. If not, have another go from the first step.

MY DOG HAS FLEAS

Bafflingly, the open strings in standard ukulele tuning are often referred to as "My Dog Has Fleas". This is odd in that neither the words nor starting letters have any connection to the names of the open strings. One suggestion is that it comes from the first four notes and lyrics of a now long-forgotten song – it certainly dates back to at least the 1920s. As a strict tuning device it's more or less useless, but if you have the bottom string (G) in tune, and you know the melody, then tuning the other three strings relative to that G becomes pretty simple. If no other instruments are involved, as long as the four strings play that tune then you're in business! If you're after a mnemonic reminder of the note names, though, then "Goats Can Eat Anything" is a pretty easy one to remember.)

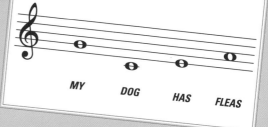

MY   DOG   HAS   FLEAS

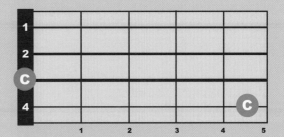

4. (Alternative) If you have a tenor ukulele and you tune the 4th string to low E, then play the 5th fret of the 4th string and adjust the pitch until it matches the open 3rd string.

Your First Chords

Now it's time for you to make some music. We'll begin with a couple of simple chords — F and C … well, technically we should call them F major and C major. Using these two chords, you'll be able to strum along to your first tune. And then we'll add a few more chords on top. By the end of this section you'll be able to play the ukulele… a bit.

Finger position for an open C major chord.

Playing C Major

This chord really is just about as simple as it could be. You're going to put one finger on one string and then strum across all four of them with your other hand. In fact, if you just play the bottom three strings alone, that will give you the three notes that make up the C major chord – G, C and E. It's difficult, though, to strum the ukulele on just three strings without accidentally hitting the other, so by positioning your 3rd finger (or ring finger) on the 3rd fret of the top string you now have a second C note – in this case, one octave higher than the open 3rd string. Now you can play all four strings. Let's try it out.

1. Fret the note following the photograph and diagram on this page. That's using your 3rd finger (the number shown in the red circle) to press down on the 3rd fret of the top string.

2. Begin by just playing that string. If you've fretted the note correctly, with your finger pressing down *just behind* the fret, then you will hear a perfectly clear note; if you get a muted thud then it means you're either not holding down the string firmly enough or you are actually pressing down ON the fret, deadening the note with your finger.

3. Gently brush the strings with the nail of your index finger, starting with the 4th string and working across to the 1st. If it sounds unpleasant, check again that your finger is on the correct fret and string.

C MAJOR (C)

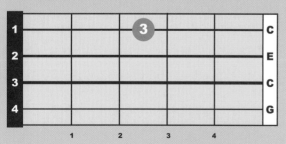

Notating Chords

This is a good opportunity to introduce notation and TAB. As we've already said, it's not absolutely necessary to learn how to read music but the TAB will certainly be helpful because it provides explicit instructions about which string and fret to use. In the box on the right you can see the C major chord you've just played written down as standard notation and as TAB. See what we mean about TAB being very simple? It *literally* is a fingerboard diagram. Because of the ukulele's unique "re-entrant" tuning (the bottom string not being the lowest pitched note), standard notation is less useful for writing down ukulele chords, but it's universality makes it the most appropriate form for showing melodies.

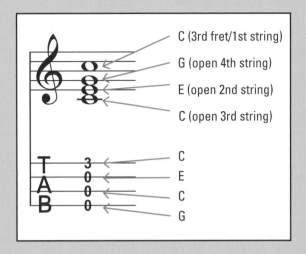

Notation and tabulation for an open C major chord.

Playing F Major

Let's follow that chord with a slightly more demanding example. F major requires you to use two of your left-hand fingers to fret the notes.

1. Begin by taking your 1st finger and placing it on the 1st fret of the 2nd string (the E string). This produces the note F.

2. Now take your 2nd finger and place it on the 2nd fret of the bottom string (the G string). This will produce the note A.

3. Strum across all four strings.

Playing this chord can be a little tricky at first because you have to fret notes on the 2nd and 4th strings WITHOUT accidentally muting the open C of the 3rd string. The best way to avoid this is to ensure that the tips of your fingers are touching the strings as close as you can manage to a ninety-degree angle.

This chord also illustrates one of the unsatisfactory ambiguities of using standard notation with the ukulele. The note A is played on the top and bottom strings. Unlike the C major chord, which doubled up the note C

F MAJOR (F)

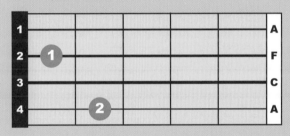

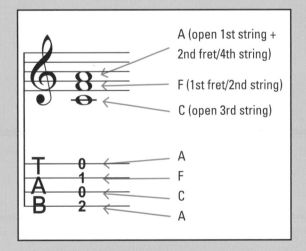

Notation and tabulation for an open F major chord.

an octave apart, the two As are the same pitch, and so are only shown once in the notation.

NOTE VALUES

Every note on the staff indicates two basic musical characteristics. We already know how its position on the staff describes the name, and therefore pitch, of the note. It also shows its duration – in other words, how long the note should play. In written music we can interpret this from looking at the notes on the staff, which are shown as multiples or subdivisions of a single beat.

In the examples on the right we can see from the time signature that there are four "beats" in every bar of music. The basic "currency" of a four-four time signature is four crotchets in each bar. If you look at the bar of crotchets, the note is played on every beat; if you count the beats out loud that means playing the note on "one", "two", "three" and "four". On the bar above you'll see that each minim lasts for two beats, so the note is played on a count of "one", sustained through "two", the next minim is played on "three" and sustained through "four". Similarly, on the semibreve bar the note starts on the first beat and lasts for all four beats. For quavers, the beat has to be divided. This can be illustrated by inserting "and" between each number when you are counting. Semiquavers halve the beat one stage further, so four notes of equal value are played during each beat. As you can see on the right, these subdivided beats can be shown either as single notes with "tails" on the stems or they can be joined together with horizontal lines called "beams".

Note values can be altered by placing a dot after the head (circle) of the note. This has the effect of increasing the length of that note by half of its value. So whilst a minim lasts for two beats, a "dotted minim" lasts for three. Each type of note also has its own equivalent "rest", an instruction to play nothing for a set duration.

Moving Between Chords

Getting your fingers working so that you can move smoothly from one chord to another is one of the hardest things to do when you first learn the ukulele. In a moment we'll attempt to strum our first tune – the famous old children's clapping song, 'Skip to My Lou'. Before we try that out let's just take some time to get used to changing from one chord to the other. The C and F major chords are quite neat in that they use different fingers for fretting, making it a little easier. Look at the simple chord chart below. Slowly and evenly count out "1–2–3–4" repeatedly. Your task here is to strum each chord **downwards** (from the bottom to top strings) on each beat you count. So you play F four times, C four times, F four times, C two times and F two times. You're almost ready to play your first song!

F	/	/	/	C	/	/	/	F	/	/	/	C	/	F	/
1	2	3	4	1	2	3	4	1	2	3	4	1	2	3	4

'Skip to my Lou'

Let's put all of that together now. Here is the music for 'Skip to my Lou', along with the lyrics. To make things easier, the chord names are shown above every beat of the bar so you know when to play and when to change. For now, just strum down with your index finger on the beat… and sing along. The other verses (shown on the right) all follow the same pattern. In between each one there's a chorus that goes "Skip, Skip, Skip to my Lou".

1. Fly in the buttermilk, Shoo, fly, shoo.
2. There's a little red wagon, Paint it blue.
3. I lost my partner, What'll I do?
4. I'll get another, As pretty as you.
5. Can't get a red bird, Jay bird'll do.
6. Cat's in the cream jar, Ooh, ooh, ooh.
7. Off to Texas, Two by two.

Strumming Patterns

Playing rhythmic patterns is at the very heart of ukulele music. Creating these rhythms requires different types of strumming – after all, it would be pretty dull if we just strummed every song on the beat. You've already strummed down using your index finger to play from the bottom string to the top. These downstrokes can be alternated with upstrokes, where you use the pad of your index finger to strum up from the 1st string to the 4th. The downstroke is usually played directly after an upstroke – since the finger is already in the correct position. There is a subtle difference in the way these strokes sound. You can hear it if you play 'Skip To My Lou' first using all downstrokes and then alternating with upstrokes on the second and fourth beats.

Below you'll find eight strumming patterns for you to try out. On each staff we've shown "slash" noteheads that are used for notating rhythm. While you play, count out the beats, remembering that the quavers are half beats (one-and-two-and…"). And,

of course, pay special attention to the direction of the stroke. You can use these patterns for most of the songs shown throughout the book. Of course, you don't have stick with one pattern, you can vary them within the same song.

Play 'Skip to My Lou' using each of the different patterns. Listen to the difference – it really can bring a song to life. The key to strumming the uke is keep your wrist loose and relaxed – that's where the movement is coming from rather than the fingers and thumbs. The stroke direction is shown beneath the staff – "D" is a downstroke; "U" is an upstroke.

The bottom two examples are reggae and ska rhythms, which both include rests. In the bottom-left (reggae) example you play nothing on beats "1" and "3". The ska rhythm (bottom right) only plays on the off-beat – the staff shows a semiquaver rest on each beat so you only play on "and". Although we've suggested downstrokes, try it out again, this time only using upstrokes.

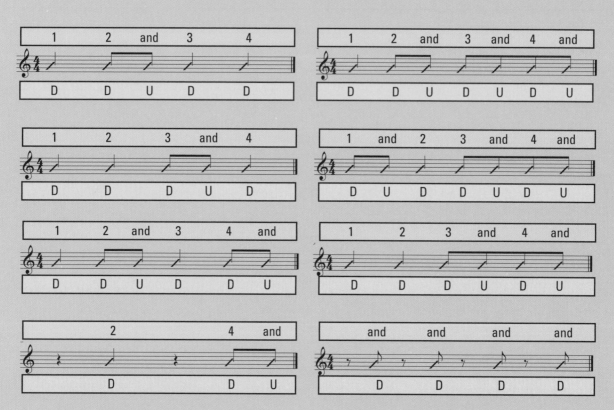

'Cotton-Eyed Joe'

Now we'll start to build up a bit more of a chord vocabulary. 'Cotton-Eye Joe' is an American folk tune that dates back to before the Civil War. This version will use three new major chords in the keys of D, G and A. Two of these chords will be a little tricky for beginners as they make use of a third finger. (Even the least eagle-eyed of guitar players out there will recognise these shapes as A, D and E on the top four strings.)

The chords you need to play are written above the music, and aligned with the beat. You keep playing that chord until instructed otherwise.

Finally, just a note on the music. You'll see there are two sharp symbols before the four-four time signature. This tells you that the song is in the key of D. The scale of D major goes D–E–F#–G–A–B–C#–D, and so to prevent the staff becoming a mess of sharps they are placed at the beginning to indicate that all notes on the C or F positions on the staff are C# and F#. We'll cover scales in a little more detail later in the book.

D MAJOR (D)

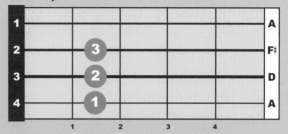

G MAJOR (G)

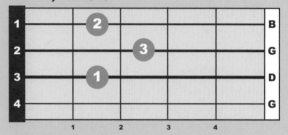

A MAJOR (A)

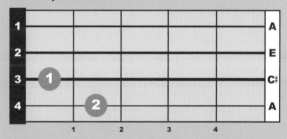

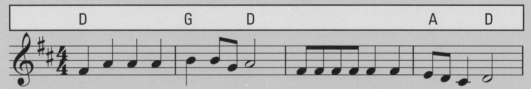

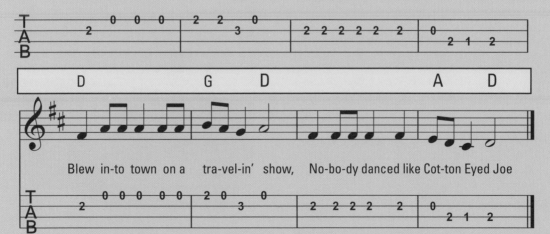

Barre Chords

Let's look at another major chord. B♭ major (or C♯ major as it could also be named) is one of the most difficult open-string chords because it requires you to use your 1st finger to cover two strings. The is called a partial barre (pronounced "bar").

Start by getting the 2nd and 3rd fingers into position on the 3rd and 4th strings. Now lay your 1st finger over the top two strings.

The two main difficulties you'll have with this chord will be in applying enough pressure from the 1st finger to fret the notes, and also keeping it broadly parallel with the fret. If you fail to do these, one or both of these strings are likely to be muted. There's a second way of playing this chord. The same notes are fretted in the same positions, but this time a full barre is created by placing the index finger across all four strings.

Moving Barre Chords

The B♭ major is an interesting chord shape because it introduces the idea of mobility along the fingerboard. If we take that shape – regardless of whether we use a partial or full barre – and play it at different positions we can, in effect, use it to play any major chord.

We can illustrate this by moving the B♭ shape two frets along the fingerboard. This now produces a C major chord. Play it a few times and then compare it to the open C major you already know. Although the chord contains the same notes, the sound is quite different because on the bottom three strings the notes are played at different positions and have a different emphasis. For example, some players prefer this version of C major because the notes are closer together – the open C has quite a big gap in pitch between the two top strings which can sound a little thin.

Using this shape, the chord can be named after the note on the top string of the index-finger barre.

B♭ MAJOR

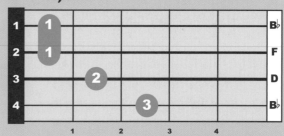

B♭ major partial barre

B♭ major full barre

C MAJOR

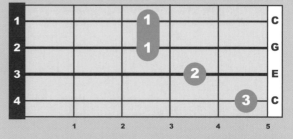

C major partial barre

Time Signatures

All of the songs we've worked through so far have been in what is known as four-four time. As you've seen, the characteristic of this time signature is that the music is contained within bars of four beats. But not all music works in this way. Another widely used time signature is "three-four", which is also known as "waltz time" because of the dance. It is indicated in music notation with the number 3 above the number 4 at the beginning of the staff. And this means that each bar consists of three crotchet beats. If you count out a repeating sequence of "one-two-three", emphasising the first beat, you'll quickly be able to get the feel of this time signature.

Here's and example for you to try out, the folk song 'On Top of Old Smokey'. This version only uses the chords F, C and G major, but this time we'll use the barred C major shown across the page. This will be useful in getting you accustomed to moving between the barre shapes and the open chords. (To get to grips with the song and the timing to begin with, you can use the regular open C major if you like.) Note: between bars 7 and 8 you will see two notes linked together by a curved line. This is a "tie" and is used to sustain notes over the end of a bar. So in this case, you play the dotted minim (three beats) but sustain it over the three beats of the following bar.

Chucking and Muting

Strumming out chords on the ukulele using downstrokes and upstrokes will produce clean, ringing, sustaining chords. And that's nice. But it's also possible to create more rhythmic interest by adding percussive strumming effects to the brew. To get the idea, try fretting any open-string chord and then, before you pick the notes, hold the palm of your right hand over the strings. You can *kind of* hear the chord but you'll mostly be aware of the sound of your fingernail making contact with each of the strings.

One muting technique commonly used when creating rhythms is referred to as the "chuck". Integrating muting with different strokes, the term that does perfectly describe the sound it makes.

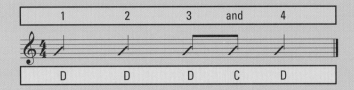

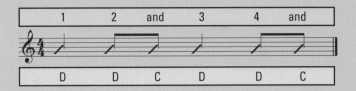

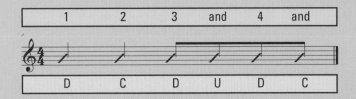

1. Begin by forming a G major chord (see page 33 if you need a reminder).

2. Strum a single downstroke in the usual way.

3. Follow this with an upstroke, but the moment you've made contact with the strings, deaden them by pressing the palm of your right hand across all of the strings. You should still be able to hear the chord underneath the percussive thwack.

Chucking can be used effectively with upstrokes and downstrokes, and is an important component of that characteristic "chukka" rhythm heard on so many ukulele recordings.

Try strumming some of rhythms on page 32, which have now been adapted: the chuck is marked in the stroke directions with a "C".

Adding a Little Swing

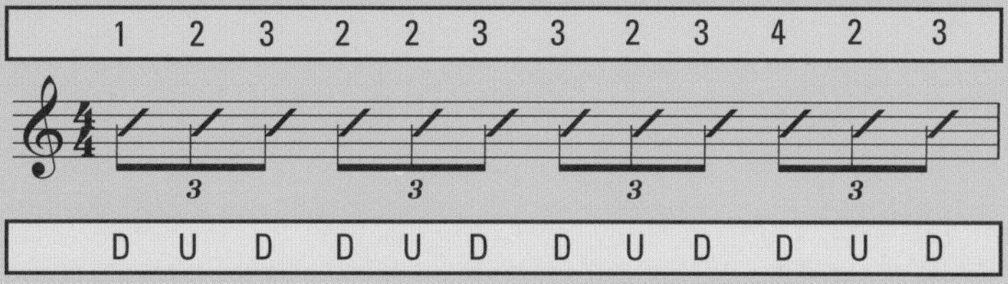

The strumming patterns we've worked on so far have been strictly on the beat or the half-beat. It's far more common, though, to strum with a "swing". The effect of playing with a swing is quite difficult to describe; it's best illustrated using music notation but even this is really an approximation. It's all about getting the right "feel".

The first staff shown here (top right) contains one bar of four-four time, where each crotchet beat has been divided into three "tuplets" – these are notes joined by a beam with the number "3" to identify the subdivision. To hear how this works, count "1–2–3–4" on the beat, and then insert "2–3" between each beat. So your count will be "1–2–3–2–2–3–3–2–3–4–2–3"; if you emphasise the first beat of each set of tuplets you'll quickly get the idea. Try it out on a G major chord using the stroke instructions underneath the staff.

1	2	3	2	2	3	3	2	3	4	2	3

D U D   D U D   D U D   D U D

1	2	3	2	2	3	3	2	3	4	2	3

D   U   D   U   D   U   D   U

Din - ga   Din - ga   Din - ga   Din - ga

1	2	3	2	2	3	3	2	3	4	2	3

D   U   C   U   D   U   C   U

Din - ga   Chuk - ka   Din - ga   Chuk - ka

In the second example (above centre), the second note of each set of tuplets has been replaced by a rest. This time, count out the same beat but emphasise all of the notes: "1-2-3-2-2-3-3-2-3-4-2-3". Now try to play the G major chord using that rhythm. Notice that the strumming pattern plays downstrokes on the beat and upstrokes on the tuplet before the beat.

The third example (above bottom) replaces downstroke in the second and fourth tuplet sets with a chuck. And this is perhaps the most characteristic of all ukulele strumming patterns.

As a reminder, some players like to give names that mimic the rhythm of their strumming patterns. So in this way the second example could be called a "dinga-dinga" rhythm, and the third a "dinga-chukka"

LEFT-HAND MUTE

Instead of "palming" the strings, a gentler alternative method of muting uses the fingers of the left hand to stop the strings vibrating. To do this you simply release the pressure of the fretting fingers after you've played the notes. This is a more controlled technique that gives you the freedom to allow the strings to ring before they are muted. This is particularly effective for the last chord of a song where, for example, you might want the strings to sustain strictly over four beats before muting the sound.

'Admiral Benbow'

We'll end this section with a full song for you to play through. 'Admiral Benbow' is an English sea shanty that dates back to late 1700s. It's a simple three-chord song using G major, C major and D major. Take it at a brisk pace and try to make your chord changes as smooth as possible. If you're feeling bold, you can attempt to play the tune, which is shown on the TAB beneath. Don't worry if that's too much for now – we'll cover single-note playing later in the book – you can come back to it then.

fought all on the main you shall he - ar, you shall hear.

1. Come all you seamen bold
and draw near, and draw near,
Come all you seamen bold and draw near.
It's of an admiral's fame,
O brave Benbow was his name,
How he fought all on the main
you shall hear, you shall hear.

2. Brave Benbow he set sail
for to fight, for to fight,
Brave Benbow he set sail for to fight.
Brave Benbow he set sail
with a fine and pleasant gale,
But his captains they turn'd tail
in a fright, in a fright.

3. Says Kirby unto Wade:
"We will run, we will run,"
Says Kirby unto Wade: "We will run."
For I value no disgrace,
nor the losing of my place,
But the enemy I won't face,
nor his guns, nor his guns.

4. The Ruby and Benbow
fought the French, fought the French.
The Ruby and Benbow fought the French.
They fought them up and down
till the blood came trickling down,
Till the blood came trickling down
where they lay, where they lay.

5. Brave Benbow lost his legs
by chain shot, by chain shot,
Brave Benbow lost his legs by chain shot.
Brave Benbow lost his legs
and all on his stumps he begs,
Fight on my English lads,
'tis our lot, 'tis our lot.

6. The surgeon dress'd his wounds,
Benbow cried, Benbow cried,
The surgeon dress'd his wounds, Benbow cried.
Let a cradle now in haste
on the quarterdeck be placed,
That the enemy I may face
'til I die, 'til I die.

More Chords

Up to this point all of the music you've played has used major chords in a variety of keys. Every major chord, however, also has other equivalent chord types, all of which are related by being in the same key, and yet sound quite different. The most common of these are the minor chords, which are sometimes associated with mournful music. We'll also take a look at other commonly used chord types, such as sixths, sevenths, ninths, diminished and augmented sets.

Minor Chords

Every major chord has a minor counterpart which is formed by flattening the middle note of the major chord – taking the note down by a semitone. Let's look at an example in the key of C: The notes of a C major chord are C–E–G; if we flatten the middle note it produces a C minor chord (C–E♭–G).

Here are three minor chords for you to try.

A Minor

This is a very easy minor chord to play as it only requires you to use one finger. In chord naming shorthand, the minor is often shown by the key followed by a lower-case letter "m". Take your 2nd finger and place it on the 2nd fret of the bottom string, as shown in the diagram and photograph. Strum the chord.

A MINOR (Am)

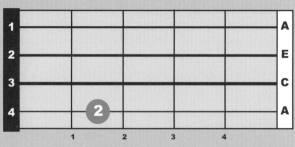

To illustrate the difference in sound between major and minor chords play the sequence shown in the TAB below. It alternates between the A major chord, which you already know, and A minor. This transition is extremely simple – all you have to do is fret the A major and then lift away your 1st finger to play A minor.

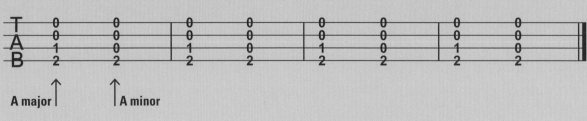

D Minor

Now we're going to repeat that exercise with a second minor chord, this time in D. Follow the instruction in the diagram: take your 2nd finger and place it on the 1st fret of the 2nd string; your 3rd finger on the 2nd fret of the 3rd string; and the 2nd finger on the 2nd fret of the bottom string. Strum the chord.

We're going to do the same major/minor exercise for the key of D, but this one is quite a bit more demanding to execute fluently because the fingering of the chord is so different. If you look at the shape of the two chords, you can see that F♯ on the 2nd string of the major chord has been flattened to an F on the minor chord. The big difference, however, is that *all* of the fingers fret different strings. This means that after you've played one chord you have to completely reposition your fingers.

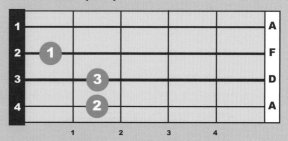

D MINOR (Dm)

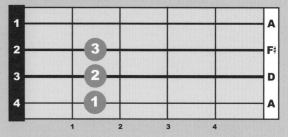

D MAJOR (D)

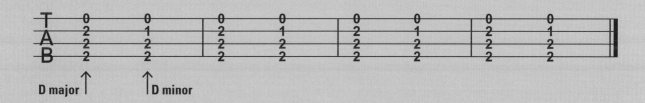

D major ↑   ↑ D minor

E Minor

The last of these chords we'll look at before you try them out in a song is E minor. It's a nice easy shape that fits the natural positioning of the three fingers: the 1st finger goes on the 2nd fret of the top string; the 2nd finger on the 3rd fret of the 2nd string; and the 3rd finger goes on the 4th fret of the 3rd string. Strum them across, including the open bottom string.

This is also a particularly useful shape as it can be adapted and used to move up and down the fingerboard, and play minor chords in any key. To do this you also need to fret the bottom string, so shift the 3rd finger across and now use the 4th finger to fret the 3rd string. If you move this shape along the fingerboard you will play a minor for the note you are playing on the 3rd string.

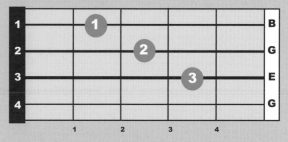

E MINOR (Em)

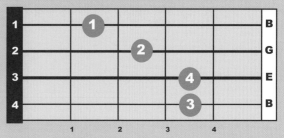

E MINOR (Em) (mobile)

'What Shall We Do With the Drunken Sailor?'

Now we'll put some of those minor chords to use with this old sea shanty that dates back to the early 1800s. The chords we need to use for this are D minor, C major, A minor and F major. Pay special attention to the swift chord changes in bars 7 and 8. You'll notice that these chords revolve around the D minor shape – all you have to do to play F is lift the 3rd finger and play the open 3rd string, or for A minor, both 1st and 3rd fingers to play the open 2nd and 3rd strings. (If you want to add the chorus, it goes "Hooray and up she rises, Hooray and up she rises, Hooray and up she rises, Early in the morning".)

Intervals

Before looking at any new chords, lets take on another little bit of music theory. This will help you to understand the way in which different chord types are created. The relationship between any two notes is referred to as an "interval". There are twelve semitones (or frets on the fingerboard) between any note and its octave equivalent. The intervals between the first note (the "tonic") and any of the others can be given a unique definition. The diagram below shows the notes starting at C, but can be applied to all other keys.

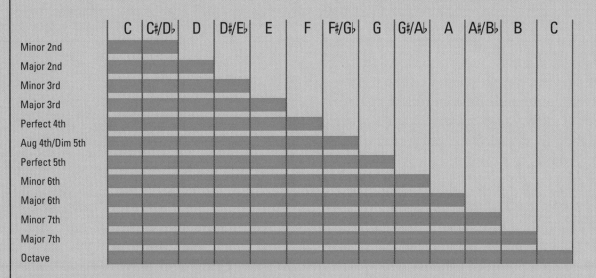

Every type of chord is defined by the intervals from the tonic. Every **major** chord is formed from a **tonic**, **major 3rd** and **perfect 5th**. That's why the notes of a C major chord have to be C, E and G. Similarly, a **minor** chord will always be formed from a **tonic**, **minor 3rd** and **perfect 5th** – in the key of C that is C, E♭ and G. Every chord type works in this way – it is defined wholly by the interval relationships of its notes to the tonic.

C Dominant Seventh

Besides the major and minor chords, the seventh is the most widely used chord type. Indeed, with these three chord types, the vast majority of pop, rock, folk and country songs can be played. A seventh chord – or dominant seventh, to give its correct name – takes the three notes of the major chord and adds a fourth note – a **minor 7th** interval. Looking at the diagram above, you can see that in the key of C that would take the notes C, E and G from the major chord and add a B♭. On the ukulele, the C7 chord is another of those super-simple shapes that requires just one finger. If you play the TAB exercise on the right, moving between C major and C7, you'll hear the difference clearly.

C DOMINANT SEVENTH (C7)

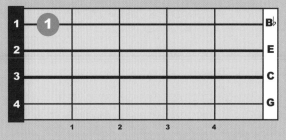

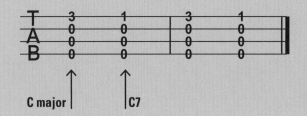

C major | C7

12-Bar Blues in Sevenths

Here are two more seventh chords. Try to play them alongside their major and minor equivalents; you'll soon begin to recognize the unique tonal character of each chord type.

Opposite, we'll use the three seventh chords you know to play a classic 12-bar-blues. This version of Bessie Smith's 'Backwater Blues' dates back to 1919 and is in the key of C, so the chords we'll use are C7, F7 and G7.

This kind of chord sequence is sometimes called a "I-IV-V" because it uses chords built on the tonic, perfect 4th and perfect 5th intervals. If you altered the key to F ("transposing" the whole thing by a perfect 4th), retaining the I-IV-V sequence, the chords would be F7, B♭7 and C7.

F DOMINANT SEVENTH (F7)

G DOMINANT SEVENTH (G7)

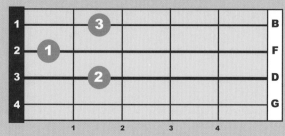

Mobile Seventh Chords

The two seventh chords shown on the right in the keys of B and D are probably the simplest barre chords you will encounter. They both require the 1st finger to cover all four strings on the 2nd fret and add the 2nd finger to the 3rd fret. As with all barre chords, these two shapes can be moved up and down the fingerboard. With the B7 shape, the top string provides the key for the chord; on the D7 shape it's the 3rd string that gives you the key.

The TAB exercise below uses both of these shapes to play the same two chords at different positions along the fingerboard. So when the D7 shape is moved along so that the barre is on the 11th fret, a B7 chord is created. Notice how different two chords containing the same notes can be.

B DOMINANT SEVENTH (B7)

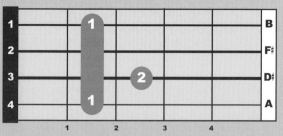

D DOMINANT SEVENTH (D7)

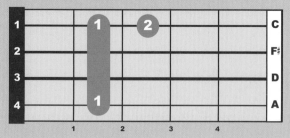

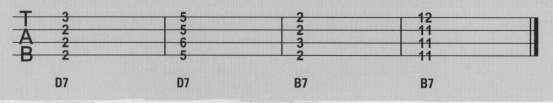

'Backwater Blues'

UKULELE CAPO

A capo is a clamping device that clips onto the neck, effectively moving the nut along the fingerboard. This is useful if you want to play familiar open-string chords in alternative keys. If you had to play a song using the chords G#, A# and D#, although this is possible, these will be among the trickier chords to finger. By fitting a capo across the third fret, you can play the simpler F, G and C open-string shapes to produce the same chords.

You'll need a small capo specifically designed for a ukulele. (A guitar capo won't work – it's just too big.) Position the top of the capo as close as possible to back of the fret and then clamp from behind the neck. The capo shown here uses a screw clamp to hold the strings tightly in place without damaging the neck.

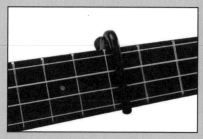

D'Addario Ukulele Capo

Open-string Chord on Capo

Major and Minor Sevenths

We'll complete our look at seventh family of chords with two more variants – the major seventh and the minor seventh chords.

The major seventh takes the three notes of the major chord and adds a **major seventh** interval. In the key of G, the notes are G (tonic), B (major 3rd), D (perfect 5th) and F# (major seventh). It's sometimes known as the "delta" chord and can be indicated in chord charts using the Greek delta symbol (△).

The minor seventh chord is built using a minor chord with an added **minor seventh**. So in G, the notes are G (tonic), Bb (minor 3rd), D (perfect 5th) and F (minor 7th). To hear the differences play all of the G chords you've encountered so far – they're shown in the TAB below.

G MAJOR SEVENTH (Gmaj7 or G△)

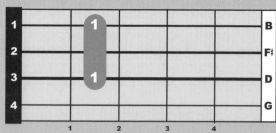

G MINOR SEVENTH (Gm7)

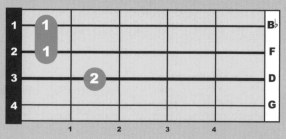

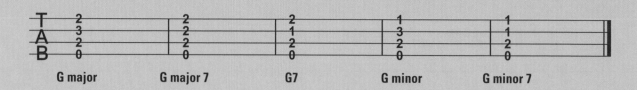

| G major | G major 7 | G7 | G minor | G minor 7 |

Sixths and Ninths

Two of the ukulele's lesser-used chord types, but that are nonetheless handy to have in your armoury, are the sixth and ninth chords.

The sixth takes the three notes of the major chord and adds a **major sixth** interval. So in the key of C, the notes will be C (tonic), E (major 3rd), G (perfect 5th) and A (major sixth). Now is the time to meet the easiest entry in the ukulele chord book. C6 requires you to use absolutely no fingering! Just play the four open strings and that's your C6. The fingering for G6 is also shown here. Alternating those two chords makes for a pleasant harmonic effect.

The ninth chord has a whole set of variations in its own right, but the one that interests us here is the dominant ninth. This chord takes the notes of a dominant seventh chord and adds a **major ninth** interval. This is an example of an extended chord, comprising a note (or notes) from beyond the octave. The major ninth is a major second beyond the octave. In the key of C, the notes of a C9 chord are C (tonic), E (major 3rd), G (perfect 5th), minor 7th (B♭) and major 9th (D).

Now it doesn't take a maths genius to see that there's a problem here: a full C9 chord requires five notes, and your ukulele has only four strings. So we have to drop one of the notes. The two chords shown here illustrate two approaches: C9 drops the perfect 5th; G9 drops the root note. To maintain the flavour of the dominant ninth chord we need to try to keep the 3rd, 7th and 9th notes. Losing the root note risks sounding "wrong" when the ukulele is the only instrument being heard, but if there are other instruments playing then they are likely to fill the hole in the chord.

Let's now play through a complete set of the chords

C SIXTH (C6)

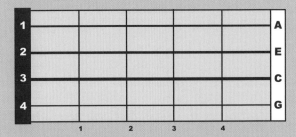

G SIXTH (G6)

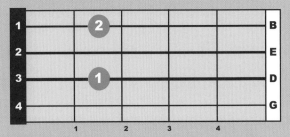

C NINTH (C9)

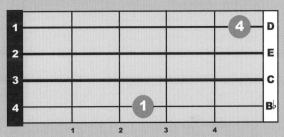

G NINTH (G9)

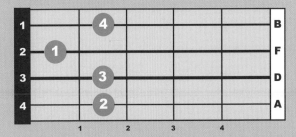

in the key of C. Take a look at the Chord Dictionary for C (page 84–85) if you need to check the correct fingering.

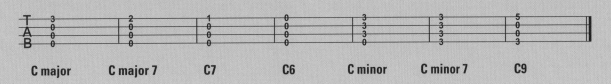

| C major | C major 7 | C7 | C6 | C minor | C minor 7 | C9 |

A FLAMENCO TOUCH

Now we're going to try a strumming technique from Andalusian flamenco playing. Known to classical guitar students as a rasgueado, this method uses the fingers to "flick" across the strings, creating a rolling effect. Let's try it out with a G major chord.

1. Hold all your fingers above and behind the 4th string.

2. Bring the 1st finger down and play across all four strings with the tip of the fingernail.

3. Bring the 2nd finger down in the same way.

4. Bring the 3rd finger down in the same way.

Once you have got the basic technique sorted, you should aim to perform all four steps in one swift movement. Rasgueado is, surprisingly, rarely used with the ukulele but it really can give added flair to your playing.

Augmented and Diminished Chords

We've already seen how the major and minor chords (or "triads" as they can be called since they comprise three notes) are at the heart of nearly all of the common chords types. There are two other types of triad that can also be used as the basis for their own family of chords. These are the diminished and augmented sets.

The diminished triad is constructed using the tonic, minor 3rd and **diminished 5th** notes. So in the key of E♭, this would be B♭ (tonic), G♭ (minor 3rd) and A (diminished 5th). We can create a diminished seventh chord from this triad by adding a **diminished seventh** interval. This is effectively a flattened minor seventh, which in E♭ is the note C.

E♭ DIMINISHED (E♭° or E♭ dim)

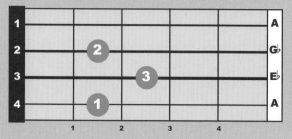

E♭ DIMINISHED SEVENTH (E♭ dim7)

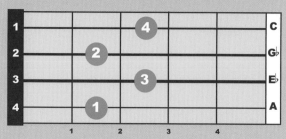

An interesting feature of the diminished seventh chord is that because of the relationship of its notes (they are all three semitones apart) you can move the shape along the fingerboard at three-fret intervals to produce chords containing the same notes. Play through the TAB on the right to see how that works.

An augmented chord takes the major triad and raises the perfect 5th by a semitone. In the key of G this means is G (tonic), B (major 3rd) and augmented 5th (D♯). Augmented chords can also be along the fingerboard at four-fret intervals.

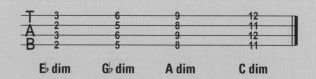

| E♭ dim | G♭ dim | A dim | C dim |

G AUGMENTED (G aug or G+)

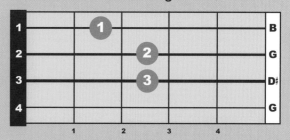

A Nice Intro

Let's tie up some of these new chords in one little phrase which, can be used as a four-bar introduction passage to a song in the key of C.

It uses the chords C6, E♭ diminished, A minor 7 and G augmented. It's shown here with an added bar of rhythm notation so you get the right swing.

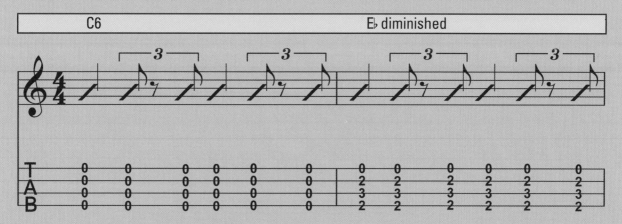

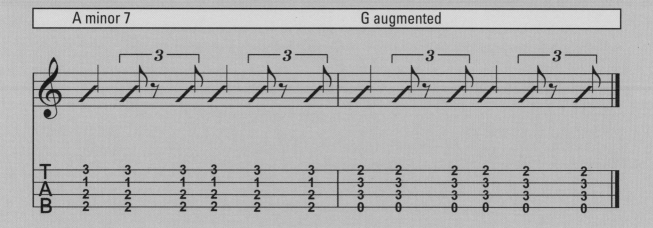

Formby Strumming

We'll end this section with some strumming patterns that are particularly associated with the great George Formby. Massively popular in Britain in the mid-20th century, he performed comedy songs backed by a ukulele (or more often a banjo ukulele). Although well-loved in the uke community, to most modern ears his tunes are certainly "of their time". Yet watching film of him performing the solos that often ended his songs, it's clear that he was an extremely skilled musician with an amazing right-hand technique.

We're going to finish this section with a look at three of Formby's characteristic strumming techniques: the triple strum, the fan and the split strum. They may look deceptively simple to play when broken down into steps but actually require a great deal of patience and practice to master at full speed. The most challenging aspect is that they integrate the fingers and thumb in a variety of alternating downstrokes and upstrokes.

When you've been playing straight alternating index finger strumming, putting the thumb in the middle will just feel awkward. The key is to begin practicing slowly until it starts to feel more natural, before you gradually up the tempo.

The Triple Strum

As the name suggests, this technique breaks down the beat into tuplets. Begin by counting out "<u>1</u>–2–3–<u>2</u>–2–3–<u>3</u>–2–3–<u>4</u>–2–3" emphasising the underlined number. The complete three-step triple strum "roll" is played for each group of tuplets. For this exercise play a standard open-string F major chord.

1. Strum DOWN across all four strings with the index finger (on the count of "1").

2. Follow through by strumming DOWN across all four strings with the thumb (on the count of "2").

3. Strum UP across all four strings with the pad of the index finger (on the count of "3").

The most difficult aspect of all of these Formby strumming techniques is making the final upstroke with the index finger after the downstroke with the thumb.

The Fan

Not dissimilar to the triple strum, this is a "showboating" technique, designed to look good while performing. Once again, the beat is broken down into tuplets with the complete movement played over each group. This method is highly unusual in that the 4th finger (the little finger) plays a fundamental part of the sequence. Count out "<u>1</u>–2–3–<u>2</u>–2–3–<u>3</u>–2–3–<u>4</u>–2–3".

1. Strum DOWN across all four strings with the 4th (little) finger (on the count of "1").

2. Follow through by strumming DOWN across all four strings with the thumb (on the count of "2").

3. Strum UP across all four strings with the pad of the index finger (on the count of "3").

For visual effect, Formby would fan out his fingers while strumming with the thumb (see the photograph above), and play the whole sequence with a circular movement of the hand from the wrist.

The Split Stroke

One of Formby's unique strum rhythms, the split stroke was used mainly during his banjolele solos. Although it looks complicated, once you get your head around the count it's easy to hear what's going on… although not necessarily so simple to replicate! Let's start off with a bar of quavers. A simple alternating strum would have you counting out "1–and–2–and–3–and–4–and", playing downstrokes on the beat, and upstrokes on the off beat. (See above the staff.) The split stroke breaks the bar up into groups – two sets of three and one of two – changing the count to "1–2–3–1–2–3–1–2" and the combination of strokes accordingly. Now try out the strokes shown beneath the staff, counting out the rhythm at the same time.

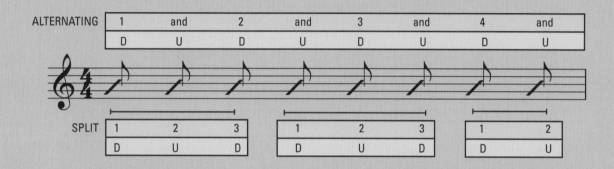

This is only part of the split stroke story, though. For the two groups of three, after each upstroke, Formby's final downstroke would not play all four strings but would just catch the 4th and 3rd strings. This not only produces a slightly percussive effect, it also cleverly changes the sound of the chord by emphasising different notes.

Split strokes were fundamental to the Formby sound as he would often create melodic effects by altering notes while playing chord – a typical example would be shifting between C major and C6 chords by taking his finger off the top string, or shifting a G7 shape down a

CI DIMINISHED 7 (CI DIM 7)

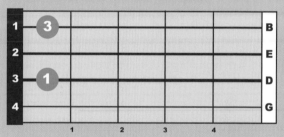

fret to form C♯ diminished 7. You can try this out for yourself using the split stroke rhythm with the TAB exercise below.

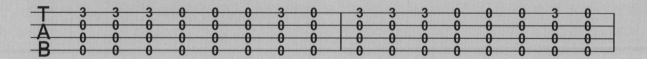

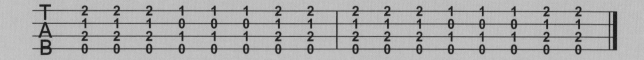

Single-Note Techniques

Traditionally, the ukulele has been used mainly for strumming chords. Playing styles have evolved, though, taking onboard single-note melodic techniques more closely associated with the guitar.

Finger Picking

We're going to focus on picking out the individual notes using the thumb and fingers in a manner that should be quite familiar to anyone who has had lessons in classical guitar. (We will give a brief mention to using a pick as this is the most effective way for playing melodies and lead runs at a high speed.)

There are three different approaches we can take for finger-picking the ukulele. We can call them "thumb only", "thumb and two fingers" and "thumb and three fingers". We'll try each one out using the notes of a C major scale. (Don't worry if you don't know what that means right now – just think of the famous 'Doe, a Deer' song from the *Sound of Music*!)

The three different techniques are each shown in the photographs on the right. In the first picture (top right) the thumb of the right hand is used to pick all of the notes. Purist pickers will scorn this idea because it does preclude playing fast runs, but if it's just very simple melodies you have in mind then it has the advantage of consistency of attack, tone and volume, which can take time to regulate between the thumb and fingers when you're starting out.

For the thumb and two fingers technique (bottom right) the thumb is used to play the 4th and 3rd strings, the index finger plays only the 2nd string and the 3rd finger plays only the top string. Guitarists with finger-picking experience will find using technique the most

Picking with the thumb.

Picking with the thumb and two fingers.

natural as they will be accustomed to using their thumbs to play the lowest note – the open 3rd string on the uke. This is arguably the best approach to playing single notes and melodies as these will mainly be played on the top three strings. The high pitch of the 4th string – being only one tone above the 1st string – makes it largely redundant for this purpose. (The exception here is for tenor ukulele players who choose a low G for the bottom string, which naturally extends the range of possible notes.)

Trickiest for beginners, the final technique (right) exclusively devotes the use of the thumb and first three fingers to each of the four strings (from bottom to top respectively). This is really more useful for integrated finger picking, such as creating arpeggio patterns when playing chords.

Picking a C Major Scale

So let's pick out that C major scale in ascending sequence – from the low C on the 3rd string to the high C on the 1st string. We won't worry about which fingers to use for fretting the strings on this exercise – just use your index finger for now. The fingerboard diagram on the right shows you the string and fret positions you need to play, beginning with the open 3rd string. The music is written below with the ukulele TAB underneath. The three rows of letters indicate the fingers to use for each of the three techniques. So begin by playing all of the notes of the scale with the thumb, as shown in the top row. When you get to the end, repeat the scale in reverse – moving from the high C down to the low C. When integrating the thumb and

Picking with the thumb and three fingers.

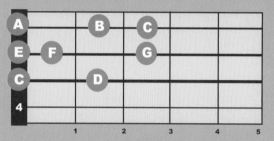

The notes of the C major scale on the top three strings.

fingers, as shown on the bottom two rows, make sure that you pick each string with the same force, keeping the volume the same from string to string.

Do	Re	Mi	Fa	Sol	La	Ti	Do
T	T	T	T	T	T	T	T
T	T	1	1	1	2	2	2
1	1	2	2	2	3	3	3

One Finger Per Fret

When playing that C major scale, you may have noticed that just using one finger to fret all of the single notes feels awkward – and if you want to play at any great tempo then it's impossible. So we'll invoke the "one-finger-per-fret rule", which enables sequences of single notes to be played more efficiently.

Let's take another look at the C major scale, only this time we'll use the correct left-hand fingering. This means that regardless of which string is being played, the notes on the 1st fret are held down by the 1st finger, notes on the 2nd fret by the 2nd finger, and notes on the 3rd fret by the 3rd finger.

Try the three picking exercises from the previous page once again, only this time using the correct left-hand fretting fingers, as shown in the photograph and diagram below.

Patterns in Motion

The one-finger-per-fret rule can be tricky at first as you have to get those fingers working independently of one another. The real value of playing in this way, though, comes when you start using sets of notes further along the fingerboard.

To illustrate this idea, we'll play another major scale, this time in the key of F. It will use the same pattern of notes only they will be shifted along the fingerboard by five frets. This will be considerably tougher because your "pinky" (4th finger) has to be called into action; since that finger generally gets such little use the muscles may initially refuse to follow your orders.

The photograph and diagram below shows the fingering for the F major scale. Try it out using the three different picking techniques. The notation and TAB for the scale is shown at the top across the page.

Fretted by 1st finger   Fretted by 2nd finger   Fretted by 3rd finger

C major scale fingering

Fretted by 1st finger   Fretted by 2nd finger   Fretted by 3rd finger   Fretted by 4th finger

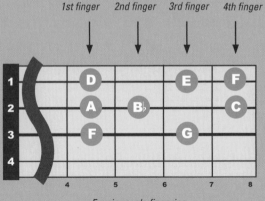

F major scale fingering

	Do	Re	Mi	Fa	Sol	La	Ti	Do
TAB	5	7	5	6	8	5	7	8
	T	T	T	T	T	T	T	T
	T	T	1	1	1	2	2	2
	1	1	2	2	2	3	3	3

G Major Scale

Using this pattern of notes, by shifting your entire left hand along the fingerboard it becomes possible to play a major scale in any key. For example, by moving the hand a further two frets along the fingerboard, beginning on the 7th fret, the same pattern will produce a G major scale (see below).

| Fretted by 1st finger | Fretted by 2nd finger | Fretted by 3rd finger | Fretted by 4th finger |

G major scale fingering

MORE SCALES

Playing scales at different positions may not seem like the greatest fun... to be perfectly honest, it really isn't. But it's SO useful if you want to play melodies on your ukulele with any fluidity. Now we're not going to show you pages and pages of scales in every key for you to work through, or even give them much of an explanation – that's not the point of this book. But if you want to be a seriously good single-note player, then you need to familiarise yourself with at least the major, minor and pentatonic scales. There are plenty of others you can investigate, though, such as diminished and augmented scales. You'll find a selection of examples are on the next two pages.

Mobile Scales

Here are seven different types of scale for you to try out. They are the major, three minors, two pentatonics and augmented scales. . It's a good practice to learn how to play them both in their ascending and descending forms – from the lowest to the highest pitch and then in reverse.

The scale patterns shown here are all in F and begin with the root note on the 3rd string. When your fingers become used to these patterns you can simply slide them along the fingerboard to play in different keys. The specific key will be defined by the lowest -pitch note on the 3rd string – this is shown on the table on the right).

MAJOR

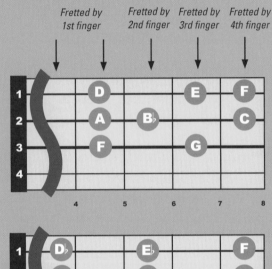

NATURAL MINOR

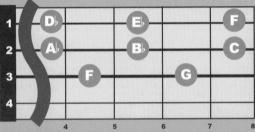

HARMONIC MINOR

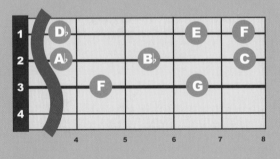

MELODIC MINOR

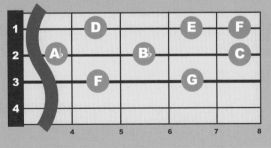

As you can see from the fingerboard diagrams, it isn't actually possible to apply the one-finger-per-fret rigidly when playing the minor scales. When this occurs, you have to use the 1st finger to cover the first two frets – this works because you never have to play both frets in succession on a single string.

(Finally, and for reasons well beyond the scope of this book, it should be noted that when you play a descending melodic minor scale, you revert to the notes of the natural minor. So in the key of F you would play F, G, A♭, B♭, C, D, E, F when ascending but F, E♭, D♭, C, B♭, A♭, G, F when descending.)

Fret	0	1	2	3	4	5	6	7	8	9	10	11	12
Key	C	C#/D♭	D	D#/E♭	E	F	F#/G♭	G	G#/A♭	A	A#/B♭	B	C

Fret position for scales beginning on the 3rd string.

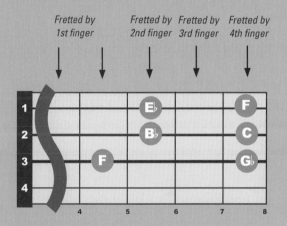

Fretted by 1st finger   Fretted by 2nd finger   Fretted by 3rd finger   Fretted by 4th finger

MINOR PENTATONIC (BLUES SCALE)

MAJOR PENTATONIC

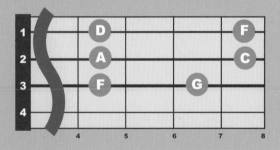

AUGMENTED

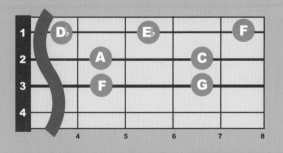

SINGLE-NOTE TECHNIQUES

Playing a Melody

Now let's combine the lessons of the last few pages by playing a simple melody. 'This Old Man' is a children's song that everyone knows, so if you're new to music notation, you can use it to get to grips with the note durations shown on page 30. To make things easier, try this exercise that uses counting and clapping.

1. The green panel above the stave shows the count of four crotchet beats in each bar. Count the numbers out loud – "one-two-three-four".

2. Counting at the same speed, now add the word "and" in between each beat – "one-and-two-and-three-and-four-and".

3. While still counting, follow the green panel and clap each time a beat (or "and" on the half beat) is underlined. Since you clap your hands every time a note is played you should recognise that you are clapping the rhythm of the tune.

4. Now try playing the tune on your ukulele. The TAB shows you which string/fret combinations to use. Since it all takes place on the first three frets, make sure that you use your 1st, 2nd and 3rd fingers to play the 1st, 2nd and 3rd frets respectively. The two panels beneath the TAB show you which fingers to use to pick the strings, first using thumb and two fingers and then thumb and three fingers below.

Picking Arpeggios

If you take a standard chord and play it as a pattern of individual notes, this is called an arpeggio or a broken chord. Begin by forming a G major chord. Now pick out the notes as shown in the pink panel below the staff, using the thumb to play the 3rd string, the 1st finger for the 2nd string and the 2nd finger for the top string. In the first bar you play the crotchet notes on every beat. In the second bar you play the same phrase as quavers, with a note on every half beat. The third bar alters the sequence in which you pick the notes.

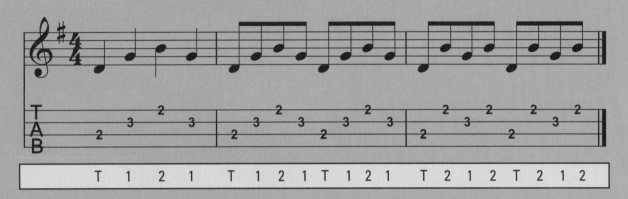

Changing Arpeggio Chords

Now we'll try out a more complex arpeggio exercise. This time you have to change chords for each bar (G major, E minor, C major and D seventh). To make things extra tricky, on the last beat of each bar you have to pick two notes at the same time – the top string with the 2nd finger and the bottom string with the thumb.

Hammering and Pulling

Let's take our single-note playing a stage further with some techniques that will enable you to play with more expression and "feel".

The *ligado*, as it's called in classical string playing, can be used to great effect with the ukulele. More commonly known as the "hammer-on", you play a note and **while the string is still ringing** you "hammer" a finger onto a fret further along the fingerboard. In effect, you are playing a second note without picking the string. Look at the two photographs on the right. The top picture shows the note D on the 2nd fret of the 3rd string being played. Notice that the 3rd finger is poised over the 4th fret ready to "hammer" (see second photograph) the note E. The instruction to hammer-on is shown in notation and TAB with the two notes joined by a curved symbol called a "slur" and the letter "H".

The reverse of this technique is called the "pull-off". Using the same two notes, the 1st finger would already be in place on the 2nd fret of the 3rd string (D), and the 3rd finger on the 4th fret of the same string (E). Play the note; while the string is still vibrating, lift the finger so that the note on the 2nd fret now sounds. (To boost the volume a little you can give the string a little "flick" as you lift the 3rd finger.) The instruction to pull off is shown in notation using a slur with a "P".

The 3rd finger is poised to hammer on the 4th fret of the 3rd string.

The finger is placed on the fret while the string is vibrating.

TRiLLS

A related musical effect, the trill is essentially super-fast alternate hammering and pulling. Using the same notes on the exercise above, play the D and very quickly repeatedly move between hammering on the E and pulling-off back to the D. If you're doing it correctly you should be able to keep the note going indefinitely.

Expressive Effects

If you think about the electric guitar – especially in rock and blues music – no solo would be complete with string bending or vibrato effects. These have both evolved as a way of trying to match the human singing voice for expressiveness. Once again, both of these techniques can be adapted for use with the ukulele.

Bending the strings, as the term suggests, entails pushing or pulling the string to the side, out of its alignment, using the fretting finger. This gradually increases the pitch of the note – in the same way as tightening the string on the tuning peg.

Using this technique on a ukulele is very different from a guitar, where the lightest strings make it possible to alter the pitch by more than an entire tone; that might be possible on the 3rd string of a ukulele, but for the other three strings a semitone is the best you'll manage. (And your fingers will get very sore trying.)

Let's look at some examples on the 3rd string, bending from the 5th fret (F) to the 7th fret (G). The various types of bends are indicated in the notation and TAB by arrows, the number at the tip indicating how far to bend – "1" indicates the pitch should be raised by a whole tone. (By the way, there are many alternative ways to show bends in notation, so you may come across other methods.)

To play the first example on the right, put your 2nd finger on 5th fret of the 3rd string. Pick the string, and while it's ringing you pull the fretting finger downward until the pitch of the note is raised by a tone. (See the photograph at the top of the page.)

In the second example, you repeat bend, only after one beat (the note is a crotchet) you slowly release the bend until it returns to its the original pitch.

The third example illustrates a 'pre-bend'. This entails bending the string into position **before** you pick the note, and then slowly releasing it so that you only hear the drop in pitch. (This one will be tricky at first as you can't actually hear if you have the bent the string by the correct amount until you pick the note – don't worry, this comes with experience.)

Vibrato

A common effect used by vocalists and string players is to end a note with fast fluctuations in pitch. This warbling effect is called vibrato. On a ukulele you can achieve this either by sliding your finger back and forth within the fret, or – less subtly – by bending the string a tiny amount using the method shown above.

The 3rd finger bends the 3rd string from an F to a G.

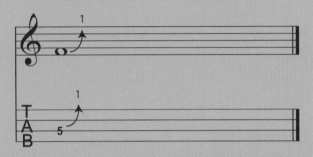

The F on the 5th fret of the 3rd string bends up by one tone.

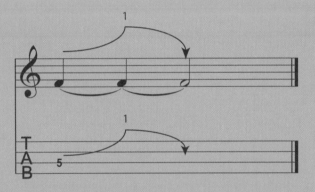

The F bends up by one tone and then back to its original pitch.

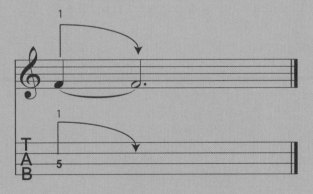

The F bends up to the G before the note is picked, and is then bent back "down" to its original pitch.

String Slides

Let's continue investigating "lead" playing effects with another really useful technique – the slide. This is a way of moving between two fretted notes by running the finger along the string.

It's a nice effect in its own right, and very characteristic of classic Hawaiian music – think of those electric lap steel guitars where a glass or metal slider is moved up and down the strings – but will also give your playing more character.

Here are three different techniques for you to try, all of which have specific musical effects – and each of which can be used to slide both up and down the string. When you slide your finger it's important to apply consistent pressure on the string against the fingerboard otherwise it will stop vibrating before you reach the second note. Equally, though, if you press too hard you will create a *glissando* effect where you'll be able to hear each note discretely along the way.

Slides on a ukulele are typically speedy, rarely lasting more than two beats. Slides are indicated in written music with a straight line between the notes, and sometimes accompanied by the letter "S". The slur (the curved line) instructs you to strike the first note and slide into the second, rather than the playing two distinct notes.

Sliding Between Two Notes

This is the most common type of slide: you fret a note and while it's still vibrating you move your finger along the string to the second note. Try the example shown below; it illustrates a slide between G and C between the 3rd and 8th frets of the 2nd string.

1. Place your index finger down on the 3rd fret of the 2nd string (G).

2. Pick the second string; while it rings, run your finger up to the 8th fret (C).

3. Now try it in reverse, playing C on the 8th fret and running the finger back down to the 3rd fret.

Sliding to a Struck Note

A similar technique, but one that produces quite a different effect, is to pick and slide, as you did in the

USING A BOTTLENECK SLIDE

For a great blues ukulele sound you can use a bottleneck slide. This is a small tube of metal or glass that fits over one of the fingers of the left hand and then placed against the strings on the fingerboard. Standard ukulele tuning means if you play the bottom three strings you can slide between major chords. (If you add the top string you can slide sixth chords.) Don't press too hard on the strings or else they may come into contact with the frets. Above all ensure that your slide runs parallel with frets or else your chords will go out of tune as you slide.

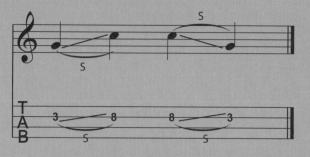

Slide between two notes

example above, but then pick the second note when you reach the correct fret. Try the exercise shown on the right. As you can see from the notation and TAB, the slur has been removed, which tells you that the second note must also be picked.

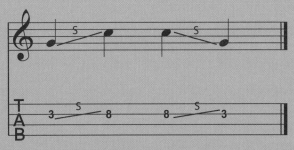

Slide to a struck note

Open Slides

Slides can also be used as a neat way of moving into and out of notes. One way of doing this is to slide into a note **before** it's been played from an indeterminate or "open" position; and you can use the same technique to slide out of a note **after** it's been picked.

To perform an open slide into a note, begin sliding on the string a few frets lower and pick the string just after you've begun sliding; when you reach the desired note let it ring. To do the reverse – to slide out – you first fret and pick the note, and immediately slide down the string releasing pressure until the sound dies away.

This type of slide is shown in written music using a short angled dash before or after the note. Below is an example for you to try out – the opening lone of 'When the Saints Go Marching In'. Sliding into the note at the

start and out at the end of the main phrase gives the melody a suitably jazzy slant.

(Note: this seems to have some tricky crotchet and quaver rests but is actually quite straightforward. In the second bar, we *could* sustain the first note for two-and-a-half beats but instead we'll slide out after one beat and then rest for one-and-a-half beats.)

Styles and Songs

Now we're going to put into practice some of the techniques shown in the previous section with a selection of songs in different styles, keys and time signatures. In common with much published ukulele music, the tune is shown in standard notation and TAB with the chord names above the staff. At the beginning of each song you'll also find the tiny "thumbnail" chord diagrams needed to play each song.

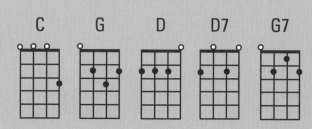

'Aloha 'Oe'

What better way to start off this section than with perhaps the most famous of all Hawaiian ukulele songs. 'Aloha 'Oe' ("Farewell to Thee") was composed by Lili'uokalani, who was the last queen to rule Hawaii before it was annexed by the United States in 1898.

As with other pieces of music in this section of the book, if you don't already know the tune then begin by carefully working it out using the notation the TAB. Start off using the most basic strumming pattern, a downstroke on every beat and gradually add some flourishes of your own. Any of the strumming patterns shown earlier in the book will work

Note: In bar six you can see that the first note (F) has been "sharpened". When one of these "accidentals" is added to a note, it remains in place for the rest of the bar. So although the third note of the bar seems to be an F, because the sharp symbol has already been applied to the first note it means that BOTH notes are played as F sharp. But AFTER the end of that bar it reverts to being an F. This is also why the sharp symbol has to be reapplied in bars 14 and 15.

STYLES AND SONGS

'In the Good Old Summertime'

This is chorus of a famous American Tin Pan Alley song that dates back to 1902.

Start off by playing downstrokes on every beat, but if you fancy a challenge, instead of just strumming try picking out arpeggios on the top three strings. As the song is in three-four time, play the 3rd string on the count of "one"; the 2nd string on the count of "two; and the top string on the count of "three".

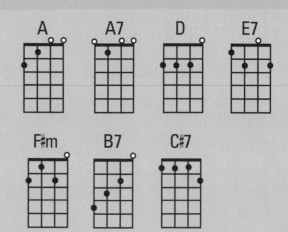

'DAISY BELL'

Variously known as 'Daisy' or 'Bicycle Built For Two', this would be a very simple waltz to perform if we hadn't excessively complicated the chords! The idea behind this is to get you changing chord shapes quickly, efficiently and smoothly, so we've put a chord change at the beginning of most of the bars – not to mention three chords in the penultimate bar that change on each beat.

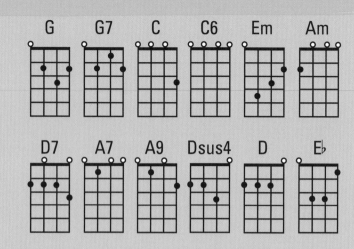

Dai - sy   Dai - sy   give me your

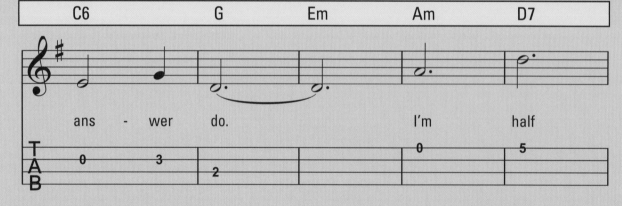

ans - wer do.   I'm   half

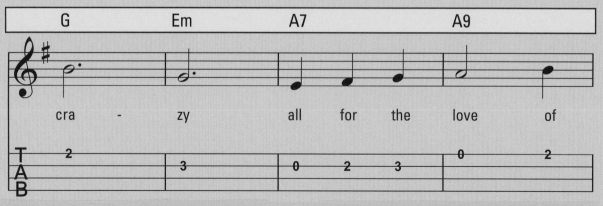

cra - zy   all for the love of

'Bill Bailey Won't You Please Come Home'

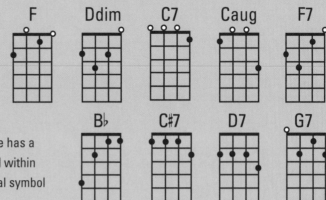

Here's a very famous early vaudeville song that was published in 1902. You can strum on the beat if you like, but a nicer alternative would be to give it a bit of Dixieland tuplet swing (see page 37). Note that in the second bar of the song the third note has a natural symbol (♮). This cancels an earlier accidental within the same bar. As the second note is an A♭, the natural symbol on the third note tells you that it reverts to A.

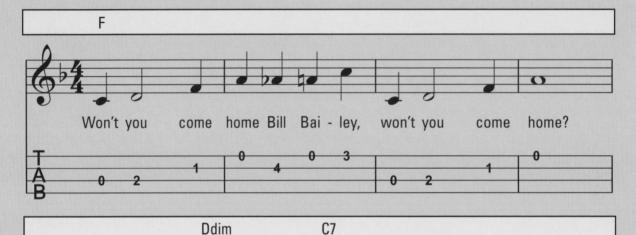

Won't you come home Bill Bai - ley, won't you come home?

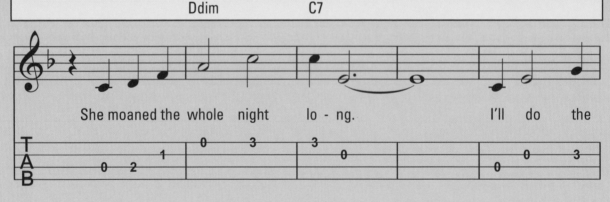

She moaned the whole night lo - ng. I'll do the

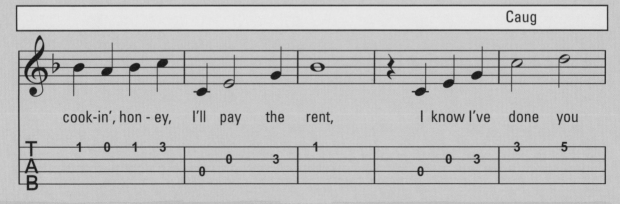

cook - in', hon - ey, I'll pay the rent, I know I've done you

STYLES AND SONGS

'Man of Constant Sorrow'

This traditional American blues-folk song dates back to the early 20th century. It uses the three-chord progression but, unusually, features a 10-bar repeating sequence, which gives it an odd sense of balance.

The version shown below shows the chords and tune. As with most blues melodies, the pitching and timing of the notes shown on the staff don't provide the full story, and allow plenty of latitude for personal expression.

To give an example, it would be quite common for the first note of the song (G) to be started a tone/step lower (F) and bent up the G during the course of the three beats. Indeed, the same approach could be taken to the first note of every bar in the song.

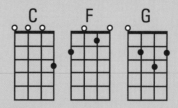

Picking Accompaniment

Let's develop 'Man of Constant Sorrow' a little further now, this time using a tricky picking accompaniment. So that you can see the music clearly, only three bars have been shown, one for each of the chords. Play each one as repeating sequence until you're comfortable. When you've mastered all three patterns you can put them together in the song. Since we're ony using the top three strings, use the thumb on the 3rd finger, and the 1st and 2nd fingers on the top two strings.

The C and G patterns both make use of hammer-on effects. In the G pattern you form the G major chord, but instead of playing D on the 2nd fret of 3rd string, you play the open 3rd string (C) and then hammer the 2nd fret.

The F pattern features a slide from E♭ to F. Play the E♭ on the 3rd fret of the 3rd string; while the note is ringing slide up to the 5th fret, but **don't** pick that note.

C Pattern

F Pattern

G Pattern

'12th Street Rag'

We'll finish off with a very simplified arrangement of a ragtime classic, '12th Street Rag', written by Euday Bowman and published in 1914. This arrangement mixes single-note runs with chords.

The Chord Dictionary

Although we've covered some melodic playing, the ukulele is nonetheless mainly used for strumming out the chords of a song. In this section we'll show you eight different chord types over all twelve keys. Each chord is also shown with two alternative fingerings, so that's almost 300 chords to learn. Using these chords, you should be able to play pretty well any song that takes your fancy.

How It Works

This is perhaps the most useful reference section of the book: indeed, anyone who knows how to play the guitar might well just head straight here and find themselves able to strum a simple set of chords within minutes. The dictionary shows each chord illustrated in four separate ways. Let's take a look at the different elements using a G Major chord.

Chord title **Chord abbreviation**

Finger number

Note name

G MAJOR (G)

String number on the nut

Fret number

The Chord Title indicates the key (**G**) and the chord type (**major**). The letters and/or symbols in brackets illustrate how the abbreviation is typically shown in a chart – if you're asked to play a "G" chord, that means that you should play a G major chord. The "enharmonic" keys (the black notes on the piano) all have two possible names: since each pair will sound identical we've described them in their most common usages – B♭, C♯, E♭, F♯ and A♭. (The alternative enharmonic names are shown in brackets.)

The Overhead Diagram depicts the fingerboard of the ukulele, showing the string numbers on the nut at the left, the fret numbers underneath, the fingers required to play the chord (shown numbered in the red circles) and the note names alongside each string on the right.

Where possible, the most common "open" versions of each chord have been shown – these are the ones that can be constructed close to the nut and usually involving at least one open string. This makes it easier when moving between chords as you won't have to keep repositioning your hand along the fingerboard. That said, on a few occasions, the most common versions of a chord will be played further along the neck – these are shown with a grey "break" line in front of the nut. In the example below, the numbering beneath the diagram tells you that frets 5, 6, 7 and 8 are used for this chord.

C DIMINISHED (C dim or C°)

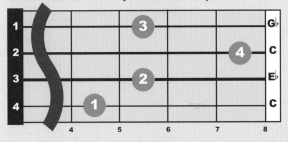

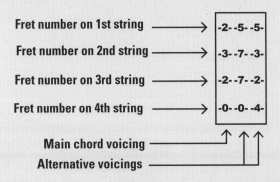

The Tablature will already be familiar to you. The first column gives you the TAB for the chord shown in the diagram to its left – so in this example the 1st, 2nd and 3rd strings play the 2nd, 3rd and 2nd frets respectively. The second and third tablature columns provide two alternative versions of the same chord but using different finger positions. (The box on the right explains more about alternative voicings.)

Standard Music Notation is shown for the basic chord. It's important to understand that this does **not** reflect the order of the notes being played on the ukulele, but the notes that **define** the chord. So for G major (see right) it shows the **tonic** (G), **major 3rd** (B) and **perfect 5th** (D) stacked up in order.

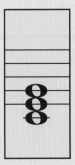

DIFFERENT VOICINGS

Any specific chord shape can be described as a "voicing". Because the ukulele has four strings it's possible to play the notes that define a chord at different positions along the fingerboard. This is why we've shown two alternative TAB voicings for each chord. In the G major example shown on the left, the note names from top to bottom are B, G, D and G. But if we look at the second voicing (the second column of tablature), this time we play the 5th fret on the 1st string, the 7th fret on the second string and the 7th fret on the 3rd string (and still play the open 4th string). The notes are "inverted" – from top to bottom they are D, B, G and G. The same notes are used but they are played at different positions on the fretboard, which means they will sound slightly different. It's actually possible to play around a dozen different variations of G major on a ukulele at different positions on the fretboard.

The Photograph gives a clear illustration of how the chord should be played, enabling you to check your own fingering.

A MAJOR (A)

A	-0-	-4-	-4-
E	-0-	-0-	-5-
C#	-1-	-4-	-4-
A	-2-	-2-	-2-

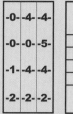 

A MINOR (Am)

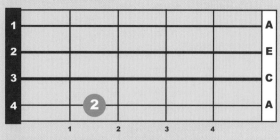

A	-0-	-3-	-0-
E	-0-	-0-	-0-
C	-0-	-0-	-0-
A	-2-	-2-	-5-

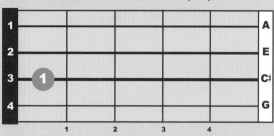 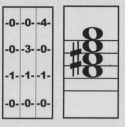

A DOMINANT SEVENTH (A7)

A	-0-	-0-	-4-
E	-0-	-3-	-0-
C#	-1-	-1-	-1-
G	-0-	-0-	-0-

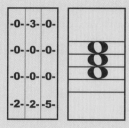 

A MAJOR SEVENTH (Amaj7 or A∆)

A	-0-	-0-	-4-
E	-0-	-4-	-0-
C#	-1-	-1-	-4-
G#	-1-	-2-	-1-

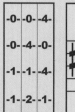 

A MINOR SEVENTH (Am7)

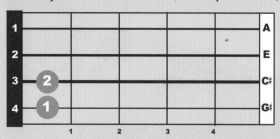

A	-0-	-0-	-3-
E	-0-	-3-	-3-
C	-0-	-0-	-0-
G	-0-	-2-	-2-

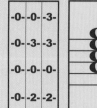 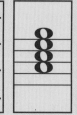

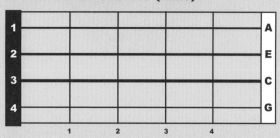

A DIMINISHED (A dim or A°)

-3-	-0-	-3-	C
-5-	-5-	-5-	A
-3-	-0-	-3-	E♭
-2-	-8-	-5-	A

A AUGMENTED (A aug or A+)

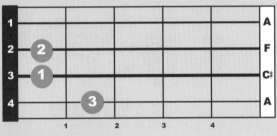

-0-	-4-	-0-	A
-1-	-5-	-5-	F
-1-	-5-	-5-	C#
-2-	-2-	-6-	A

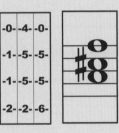

A SIXTH (A6)

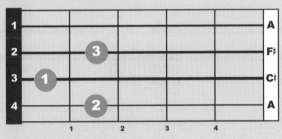

-0-	-0-	-4-	A
-2-	-0-	-2-	F#
-1-	-6-	-6-	C#
-2-	-6-	-2-	A

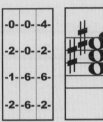

A NINTH (A9)

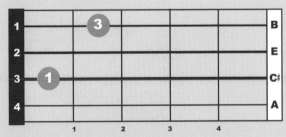

-2-	-2-	-2-	B
-0-	-3-	-3-	E
-1-	-1-	-4-	C#
-0-	-2-	-6-	A

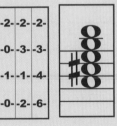

D SUSPENDED FOURTH (Dsus4)

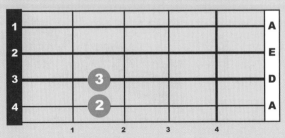

-0-	-5-	-5-	A
-0-	-5-	-5-	E
-2-	-4-	-4-	D
-2-	-2-	-7-	A

THE CHORD DICTIONARY

B♭ (A♯) MAJOR (B♭)

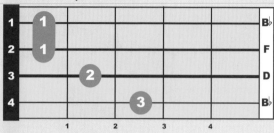

-1-	-5-	-5-
-1-	-1-	-6-
-2-	-5-	-5-
-3-	-3-	-3-

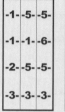

B♭
F
D
B♭

B♭ (A♯) MINOR (B♭m)

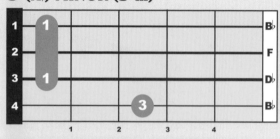

-1-	-4-	-8-
-1-	-6-	-6-
-1-	-5-	-5-
-3-	-6-	-6-

B♭
F
D♭
B♭

B♭ (A♯) DOMINANT SEVENTH (B♭7)

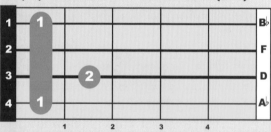

-1-	-1-	-5-
-1-	-4-	-4-
-2-	-2-	-5-
-1-	-3-	-7-

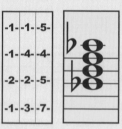

B♭
F
D
A♭

B♭ (A♯) MAJOR SEVENTH (B♭maj7 or B♭△)

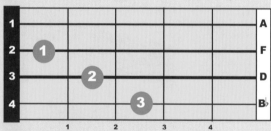

-0-	-1-	-5-
-1-	-1-	-5-
-2-	-2-	-2-
-3-	-2-	-3-

A
F
D
B♭

B♭ (A♯) MINOR SEVENTH (B♭m7)

-1-	-4-	-6-
-1-	-4-	-4-
-1-	-5-	-6-
-1-	-3-	-4-

B♭
F
D♭
A♭

B♭ (A#) DIMINISHED (B♭ dim or B♭°)

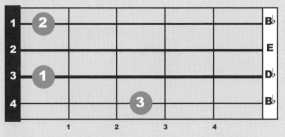

-1-	-4-	-4-
-0-	-0-	-6-
-1-	-4-	-4-
-3-	-3-	-6-

B♭
E
D♭
B♭

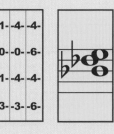

B♭ (A#) AUGMENTED (B♭ aug or B♭ +)

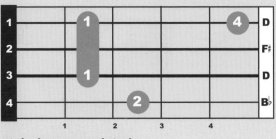

-5-	-5-	-9-
-2-	-6-	-6-
-2-	-6-	-6-
-3-	-3-	-7-

D
F#
D
B♭

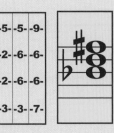

B♭ (A#) SIXTH (B♭ 6)

-1-	-5-	-5-
-1-	-1-	-3-
-2-	-2-	-2-
-0-	-0-	-3-

B♭
F
D
G

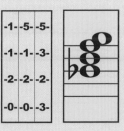

B♭ (A#) NINTH (B♭ 9)

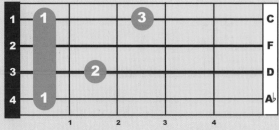

-3-	-3-	-3-
-1-	-4-	-4-
-2-	-2-	-5-
-1-	-3-	-7-

C
F
D
A♭

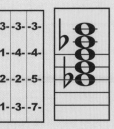

B♭ (A#) SUSPENDED FOURTH (B♭ sus4)

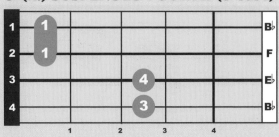

-1-	-6-	-8-
-1-	-6-	-6-
-3-	-5-	-5-
-3-	-3-	-8-

B♭
F
E♭
B♭

THE CHORD DICTIONARY

Chords in the Key of B

B MAJOR (B)

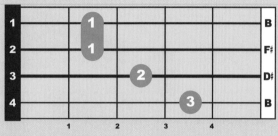   

1		1				B
2		1				F#
3			2			D#
4				3		B

-2--6--6-
-2--7--2-
-3--6--3-
-4--4--4-

B MINOR (Bm)

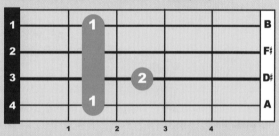 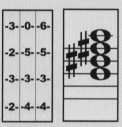 

1		1				B
2						F#
3		1				D
4				3		B

-2--5--5-
-2--2--7-
-2--2--6-
-4--4--7-

B DOMINANT SEVENTH (B7)

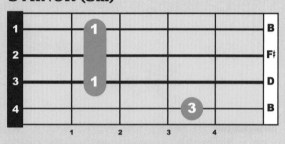 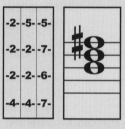 

1		1				B
2						F#
3			2			D#
4		1				A

-3--0--6-
-2--5--5-
-3--3--3-
-2--4--4-

B MAJOR SEVENTH (Bmaj7 or B△)

1	1					A#
2		2				F#
3			3			D#
4				4		B

-1--2--6-
-2--2--6-
-3--3--6-
-4--3--4-

B MINOR SEVENTH (Bm7)

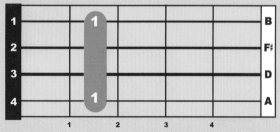   

1		1				B
2						F#
3		1				D
4		1				A

-2--0--5-
-2--2--5-
-2--2--6-
-2--4--4-

 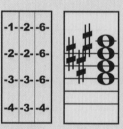 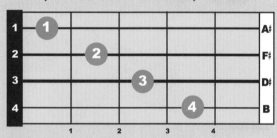

B DIMINISHED (B dim or B°)

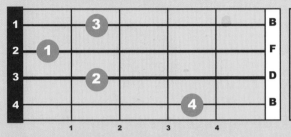

-2-	-5-	-8-
-1-	-7-	-7-
-2-	-5-	-5-
-4-	-4-	-7-

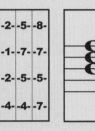

B AUGMENTED (B aug or B+)

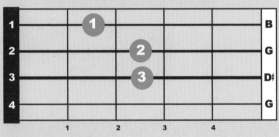

-2-	-6-	-6-
-3-	-3-	-7-
-3-	-3-	-3-
-0-	-4-	-0-

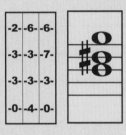

B SIXTH (B6)

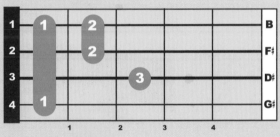

-2-	-2-	-6-
-2-	-4-	-4-
-3-	-3-	-6-
-1-	-4-	-4-

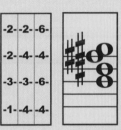

B NINTH (B9)

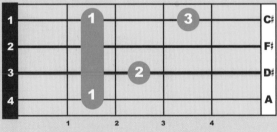

-4-	-0-	-4-
-2-	-2-	-5-
-3-	-3-	-6-
-2-	-6-	-8-

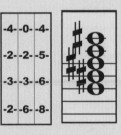

B SUSPENDED FOURTH (Bsus4)

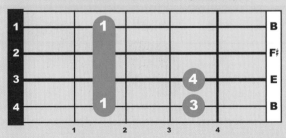

-2-	-7-	-2-
-2-	-7-	-0-
-4-	-6-	-6-
-4-	-4-	-4-

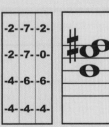

Chords in the Key of C

C MAJOR (C)

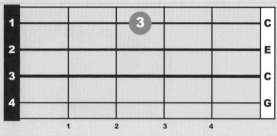

-3-	-3-	-3-
-0-	-0-	-3-
-0-	-4-	-4-
-0-	-0-	-0-

C
E
C
G

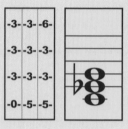 

C MINOR (Cm)

-3-	-3-	-6-
-3-	-3-	-3-
-3-	-3-	-3-
-0-	-5-	-5-

C
G
E♭
G

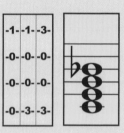 

C DOMINANT SEVENTH (C7)

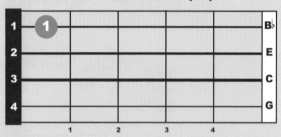

-1-	-1-	-3-
-0-	-0-	-0-
-0-	-0-	-0-
-0-	-3-	-3-

B♭
E
C
G

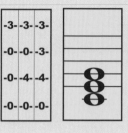 

C MAJOR SEVENTH (Cmaj7 or C△)

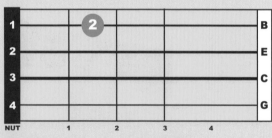

-2-	-2-	-3-
-0-	-0-	-0-
-0-	-4-	-0-
-0-	-0-	-4-

B
E
C
G

NUT

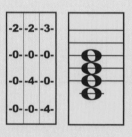 

C MINOR SEVENTH (Cm7)

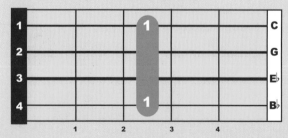

-3-	-6-	-1-
-3-	-6-	-3-
-3-	-0-	-3-
-3-	-0-	-5-

C
G
E♭
B♭

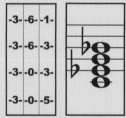 

C DIMINISHED (C dim or C°)

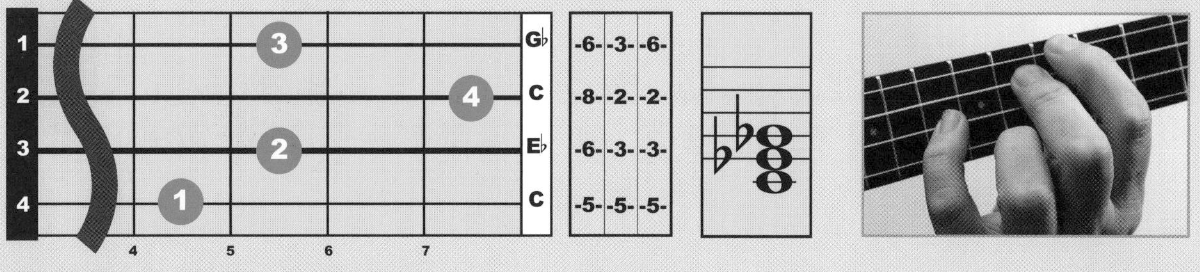

1	3		Gb
2		4	C
3	2		Eb
4	1		C

4   5   6   7

-6-	-3-	-6-
-8-	-2-	-2-
-6-	-3-	-3-
-5-	-5-	-5-

C AUGMENTED (C aug or C+)

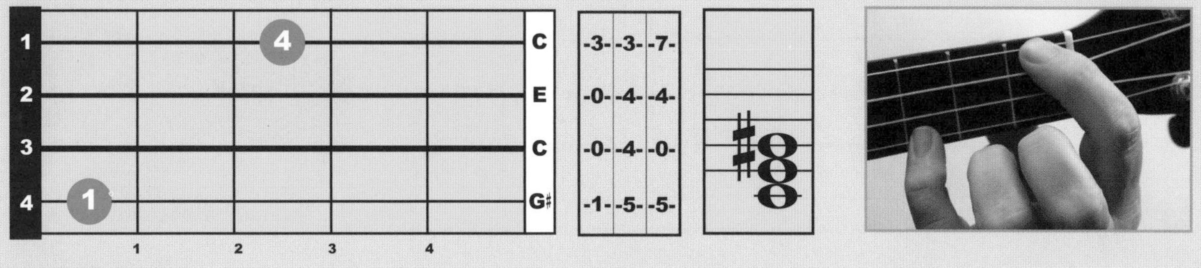

1	4		C
2			E
3			C
4	1		G#

1   2   3   4

-3-	-3-	-7-
-0-	-4-	-4-
-0-	-4-	-0-
-1-	-5-	-5-

C SIXTH (C6)

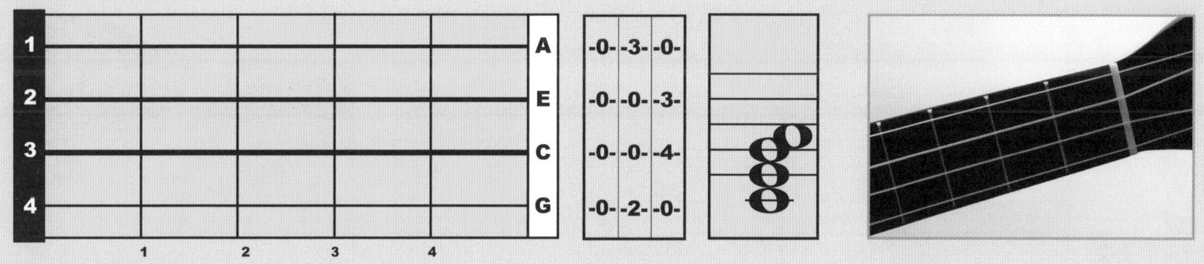

1			A
2			E
3			C
4			G

1   2   3   4

-0-	-3-	-0-
-0-	-0-	-3-
-0-	-0-	-4-
-0-	-2-	-0-

C NINTH (C9)

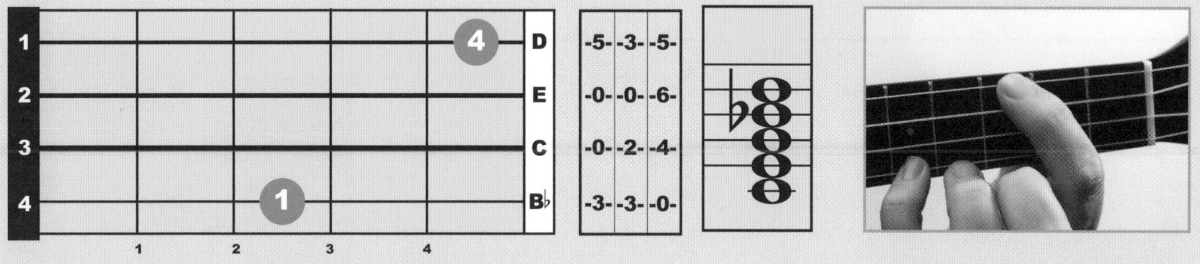

1		4	D
2			E
3			C
4	1		Bb

1   2   3   4

-5-	-3-	-5-
-0-	-0-	-6-
-0-	-2-	-4-
-3-	-3-	-0-

C SUSPENDED FOURTH (Csus4)

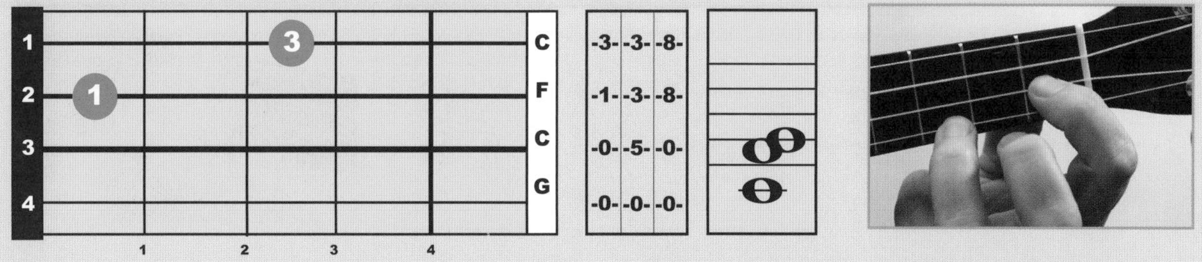

1	3		C
2	1		F
3			C
4			G

1   2   3   4

-3-	-3-	-8-
-1-	-3-	-8-
-0-	-5-	-0-
-0-	-0-	-0-

Chords in the Key of C♯/D♭

C♯ (D♭) MAJOR (C♯)

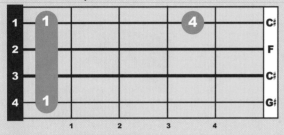

-4-	-4-	-8-	C♯
-1-	-4-	-9-	F
-1-	-5-	-8-	C♯
-1-	-6-	-6-	G♯

C♯ (D♭) MINOR (C♯m)

-4-	-4-	-4-	C♯
-0-	-0-	-4-	E
-1-	-4-	-4-	C♯
-1-	-1-	-1-	G♯

C♯ (D♭) DOMINANT SEVENTH (C♯7)

-2-	-2-	-4-	B
-1-	-4-	-4-	F
-1-	-5-	-5-	C♯
-1-	-1-	-4-	G♯

C♯ (D♭) MAJOR SEVENTH (C♯maj7 or C△)

-3-	-3-	-4-	C
-1-	-4-	-1-	F
-1-	-5-	-0-	C♯
-1-	-1-	-1-	G♯

C♯ (D♭) MINOR SEVENTH (C♯m7)

-2-	-4-	-7-	B
-0-	-4-	-7-	E
-1-	-4-	-8-	C♯
-1-	-4-	-6-	G♯

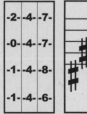

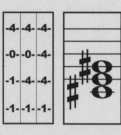
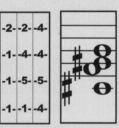
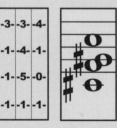

C# (Db) DIMINISHED SEVENTH (C#°)

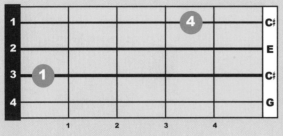
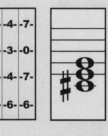

-4-	-4-	-7-	C#
-0-	-3-	-0-	E
-1-	-4-	-7-	C#
-0-	-6-	-6-	G

C# (Db) AUGMENTED (C#+)

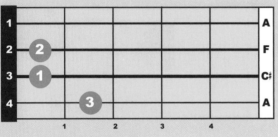
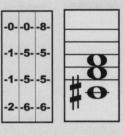

-0-	-0-	-8-	A
-1-	-5-	-5-	F
-1-	-5-	-5-	C#
-2-	-6-	-6-	A

C# (Db) SIXTH (C#6)

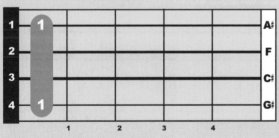
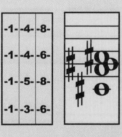

-1-	-4-	-8-	A#
-1-	-4-	-6-	F
-1-	-5-	-8-	C#
-1-	-3-	-6-	G#

C# (Db) NINTH (C#9)

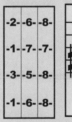

-2-	-6-	-8-	B
-1-	-7-	-7-	F
-3-	-5-	-8-	D#
-1-	-6-	-8-	G#

C# (Db) SUSPENDED FOURTH (C# sus4)

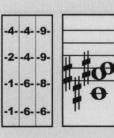

-4-	-4-	-9-	C#
-2-	-4-	-9-	F#
-1-	-6-	-8-	C#
-1-	-6-	-6-	G#

Chords in the Key of D

D MAJOR (D)

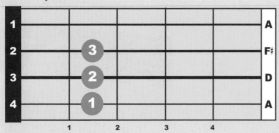

D MINOR (Dm)

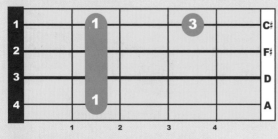

D DOMINANT SEVENTH (D7)

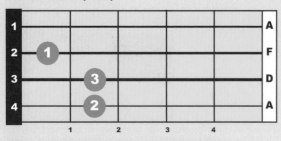

D MAJOR SEVENTH (Dmaj7 or D△)

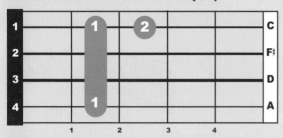
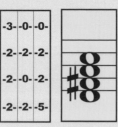

D MINOR SEVENTH (Dm7)

D DIMINISHED (D dim or D°)

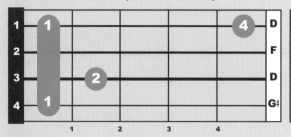

-5-	-5-	-8-	D
-1-	-4-	-10-	F
-2-	-5-	-8-	D
-1-	-7-	-7-	G#

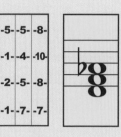

D AUGMENTED (D aug or D+)

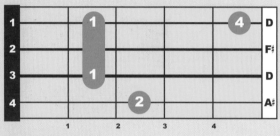

-5-	-1-	-5-	D
-2-	-2-	-6-	F#
-2-	-2-	-6-	D
-3-	-3-	-7-	A#

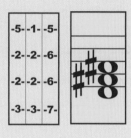

D SIXTH (D6)

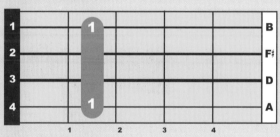

-2-	-0-	-0-	B
-2-	-2-	-2-	F#
-2-	-2-	-6-	D
-2-	-4-	-4-	A

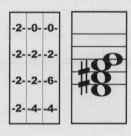

D NINTH (D9)

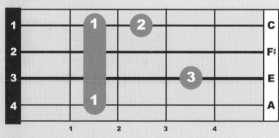

-3-	-0-	-0-	C
-2-	-0-	-2-	F#
-4-	-6-	-4-	E
-2-	-5-	-5-	A

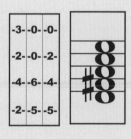

D SUSPENDED FOURTH (Dsus4)

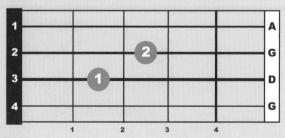

-0-	-0-	-5-	A
-3-	-3-	-5-	G
-2-	-2-	-2-	D
-0-	-2-	-0-	G

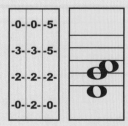

Eb (D#) MAJOR (Eb)

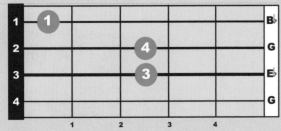

-1-	-6-	-6-
-3-	-6-	-3-
-3-	-3-	-3-
-0-	-0-	-3-

Bb
G
Eb
G

Eb (D#) MINOR (Ebm)

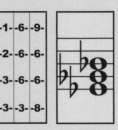

-1-	-6-	-9-
-2-	-6-	-6-
-3-	-6-	-6-
-3-	-3-	-8-

Bb
Gb
Eb
Bb

Eb (D#) DOMINANT SEVENTH (Eb7)

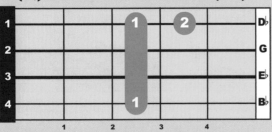
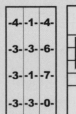

-4-	-1-	-4-
-3-	-3-	-6-
-3-	-1-	-7-
-3-	-3-	-0-

Db
G
Eb
Bb

Eb (D#) MAJOR SEVENTH (Ebmaj7)

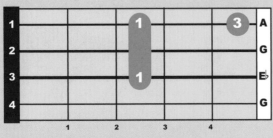

-5-	-5-	-5-
-3-	-6-	-3-
-3-	-3-	-3-
-0-	-0-	-3-

A
G
Eb
G

Eb (D#) MINOR SEVENTH (Ebm7)

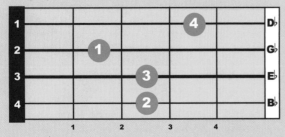

-4-	-1-	-4-
-2-	-2-	-6-
-3-	-1-	-6-
-3-	-3-	-8-

Db
Gb
Eb
Bb

E♭ (D♯) DIMINISHED (E♭°)

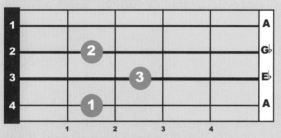

A
G♭
E♭
A

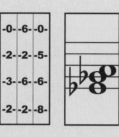

-0-	-6-	-0-
-2-	-2-	-5-
-3-	-6-	-6-
-2-	-2-	-8-

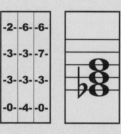

E♭ (D♯) AUGMENTED (E♭+)

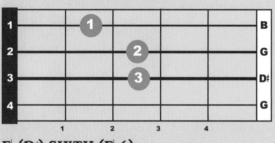

B
G
D♯
G

-2-	-6-	-6-
-3-	-3-	-7-
-3-	-3-	-3-
-0-	-4-	-0-

E♭ (D♯) SIXTH (E♭6)

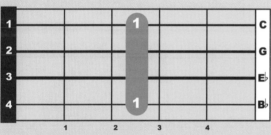

C
G
E♭
B♭

-3-	-6-	-1-
-3-	-3-	-3-
-3-	-0-	-3-
-3-	-3-	-5-

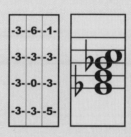

E♭ (D♯) NINTH (E♭9)

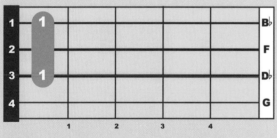

B♭
F
D♭
G

-1-	-4-	-4-
-1-	-1-	-3-
-1-	-3-	-5-
-0-	-0-	-3-

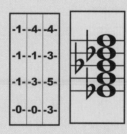

E♭ (D♯) SUSPENDED FOURTH (E♭sus4)

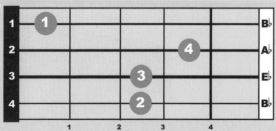

B♭
A♭
E♭
B♭

-1-	-6-	-6-
-4-	-4-	-6-
-3-	-3-	-8-
-3-	-3-	-8-

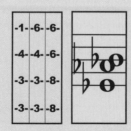

THE CHORD DICTIONARY

Chords in the Key of E

E MAJOR (E)

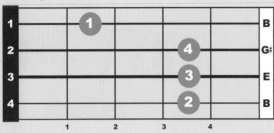

-2-	-2-	-7-
-4-	-0-	-7-
-4-	-4-	-8-
-4-	-1-	-9-

B
G♯
E
B

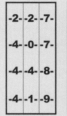

E MINOR (Em)

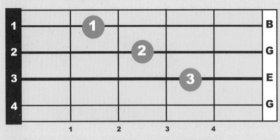

-2-	-2-	-2-
-3-	-0-	-3-
-4-	-4-	-4-
-0-	-0-	-4-

B
G
E
G

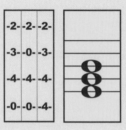

E DOMINANT SEVENTH (E7)

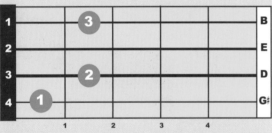

-2-	-2-	-2-
-0-	-4-	-4-
-2-	-2-	-2-
-1-	-1-	-4-

B
E
D
G♯

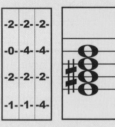

E MAJOR SEVENTH (Emaj7 or E△)

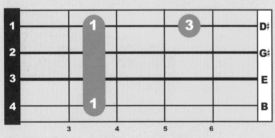

-6-	-7-	-6-
-4-	-0-	-7-
-4-	-8-	-8-
-4-	-8-	-9-

D♯
G♯
E
B

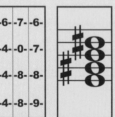

E MINOR SEVENTH (Em7)

-2-	-5-	-5-
-0-	-7-	-3-
-2-	-4-	-4-
-0-	-0-	-4-

B
E
D
G

E DIMINISHED (E dim or E°)

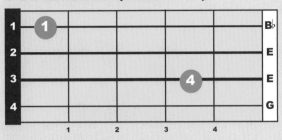

-1-	-1-	-7-	Bb
-0-	-3-	-6-	E
-4-	-4-	-7-	E
-0-	-3-	-0-	G

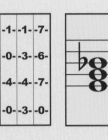

E AUGMENTED (E aug or E+)

-3-	-3-	-7-	C
-0-	-4-	-8-	E
-0-	-4-	-8-	C
-1-	-1-	-5-	G#

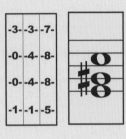

E SIXTH (E6)

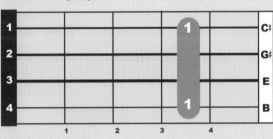

-4-	-4-	-2-	C#
-4-	-0-	-0-	G#
-4-	-4-	-1-	E
-4-	-1-	-1-	B

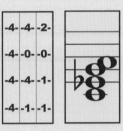

E NINTH (E9)

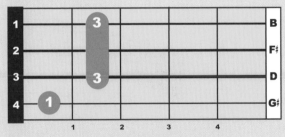

-2-	-5-	-9-	B
-2-	-4-	-7-	F#
-2-	-6-	-6-	D
-1-	-4-	-7-	G#

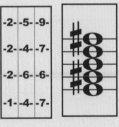

E SUSPENDED FOURTH (Esus4)

-2-	-2-	-0-	A
-2-	-0-	-5-	E
-4-	-4-	-4-	E
-4-	-2-	-4-	B

Chords in the Key of F

F MAJOR (F)

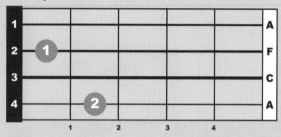

A	-0--3--0-		
F	-1--1--1-		
C	-0--5--5-		
A	-2--2--5-		

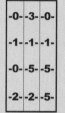  

F MINOR (Fm)

C	-3--3--8-		
F	-1--4--4-		
C	-0--5--0-		
A♭	-1--1--5-		

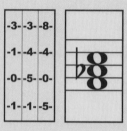 

F DOMINANT SEVENTH (F7)

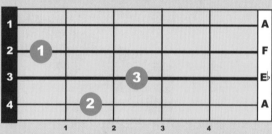

A	-0--0--6-		
F	-1--1--5-		
E♭	-3--3--0-		
A	-2--5--2-		

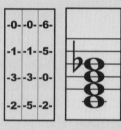 

F MAJOR SEVENTH (Fmaj7 or F△)

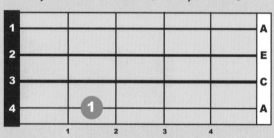

A	-0--0--0-		
E	-0--0--0-		
C	-0--5--5-		
A	-2--2--5-		

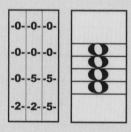 

F MINOR SEVENTH (Fm7)

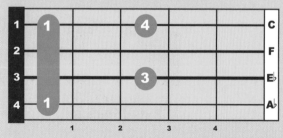

C	-3--3--3-		
F	-1--4--4-		
E♭	-3--3--3-		
A♭	-1--1--5-		

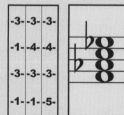 

F DIMINISHED (F dim or F°)

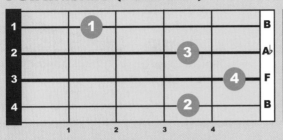

-2-	-2-	-8-	B
-4-	-1-	-7-	A♭
-5-	-5-	-8-	F
-4-	-1-	-4-	B

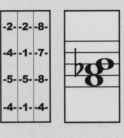

F AUGMENTED (F aug or F+)

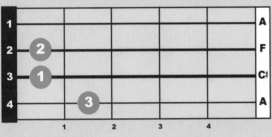

-0-	-4-	-8-	A
-1-	-5-	-9-	F
-1-	-5-	-9-	C#
-2-	-6-	-6-	A

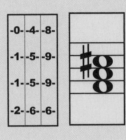

F SIXTH (F6)

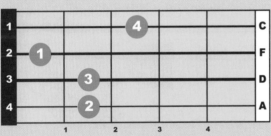

-3-	-0-	-3-	C
-1-	-1-	-5-	F
-2-	-2-	-2-	D
-2-	-5-	-2-	A

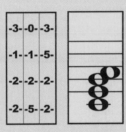

F NINTH (F9)

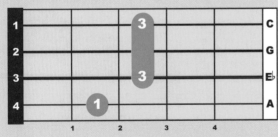

-3-	-6-	-0-	C
-3-	-3-	-3-	G
-3-	-0-	-3-	E♭
-2-	-2-	-5-	A

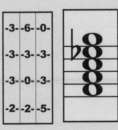

F SUSPENDED FOURTH (Fsus4)

-3-	-1-	-1-	C
-1-	-1-	-1-	F
-0-	-0-	-5-	C
-3-	-3-	-5-	B♭

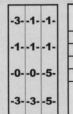
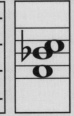

Chords in the Key of F#/Gb

F# (Gb) MAJOR (F#)

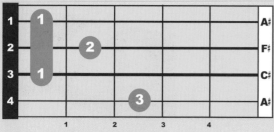

-1-	-4-	-9-	A#
-2-	-6-	-6-	F#
-1-	-6-	-6-	C#
-3-	-6-	-6-	A#

F# (Gb) MINOR (F#m)

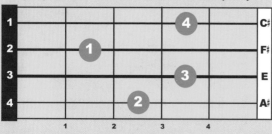

-0-	-4-	-0-	A
-2-	-2-	-5-	F#
-1-	-6-	-6-	C#
-2-	-2-	-6-	A

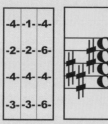

F# (Gb) DOMINANT SEVENTH (F#7)

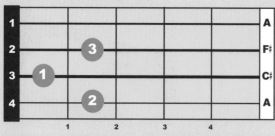

-4-	-1-	-4-	C#
-2-	-2-	-6-	F#
-4-	-4-	-4-	E
-3-	-3-	-6-	A#

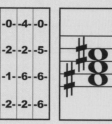

F# (Gb) MAJOR SEVENTH (F#maj7 or F#△)

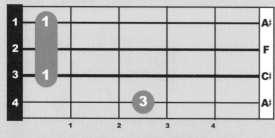

-1-	-1-	-4-	A#
-1-	-2-	-2-	F
-1-	-5-	-5-	C#
-3-	-3-	-3-	A#

F# (Gb) MINOR SEVENTH (F#m7)

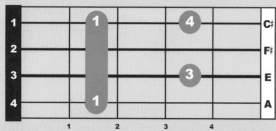

-4-	-0-	-0-	C#
-2-	-0-	-5-	F#
-4-	-6-	-4-	E
-2-	-6-	-6-	A

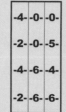

F# (Gb) DIMINISHED (F# dim or F# °)

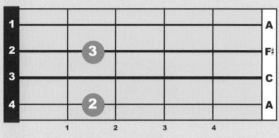

-0-	-0-	-3-
-2-	-2-	-2-
-0-	-0-	-6-
-2-	-5-	-2-

A
F#
C
A

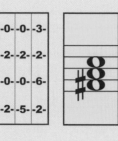

F# (Gb) AUGMENTED (F# aug or F# +)

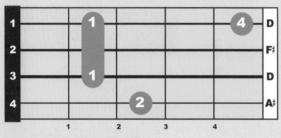

-5-	-5-	-8-
-2-	-6-	-6-
-2-	-6-	-6-
-3-	-7-	-7-

D
F#
D
A#

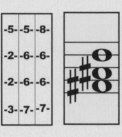

F# (Gb) SIXTH (F# 6)

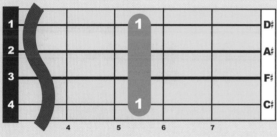

-6-	-6-	-9-
-6-	-6-	-6-
-6-	-6-	-6-
-6-	-8-	-8-

D#
A#
F#
C#

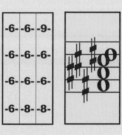

F# (Gb) NINTH (F# 9)

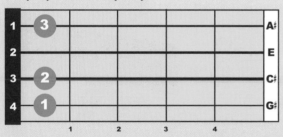

-1-	-4-	-7-
-0-	-4-	-6-
-1-	-4-	-8-
-1-	-3-	-6-

A#
E
C#
G#

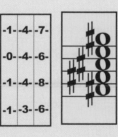

F# (Gb) SUSPENDED FOURTH (F# sus4)

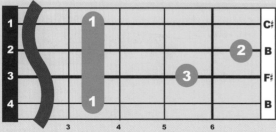

-4-	-2-	-2-
-7-	-2-	-2-
-6-	-6-	-1-
-4-	-6-	-4-

C#
B
F#
B

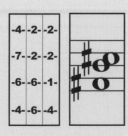

Chords in the Key of G

G MAJOR (G)

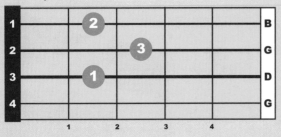
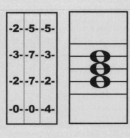

-2-	-5-	-5-	B
-3-	-7-	-3-	G
-2-	-7-	-2-	D
-0-	-0-	-4-	G

G MINOR (Gm)

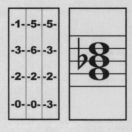

-1-	-5-	-5-	B♭
-3-	-6-	-3-	G
-2-	-2-	-2-	D
-0-	-0-	-3-	G

G DOMINANT SEVENTH (G7)

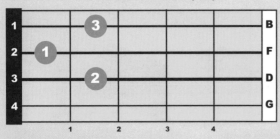
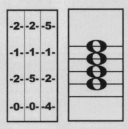

-2-	-2-	-5-	B
-1-	-1-	-1-	F
-2-	-5-	-2-	D
-0-	-0-	-4-	G

G MAJOR SEVENTH (Gmaj7 or GΔ)

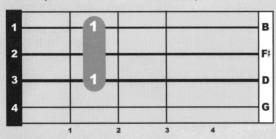
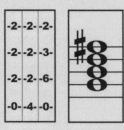

-2-	-2-	-2-	B
-2-	-2-	-3-	F#
-2-	-2-	-6-	D
-0-	-4-	-0-	G

G MINOR SEVENTH (Gm7)

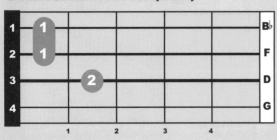
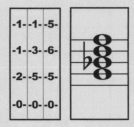

-1-	-1-	-5-	B♭
-1-	-3-	-6-	F
-2-	-5-	-5-	D
-0-	-0-	-0-	G

G DIMINISHED (G dim or G°)

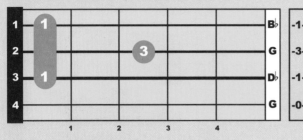

-1-	-1-	-4-	B♭
-3-	-3-	-6-	G
-1-	-1-	-7-	D♭
-0-	-3-	-0-	G

G AUGMENTED (G aug or G+)

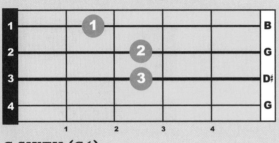

-2-	-6-	-6-	B
-3-	-3-	-7-	G
-3-	-3-	-7-	D♯
-0-	-4-	-0-	G

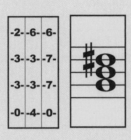

G SIXTH (G6)

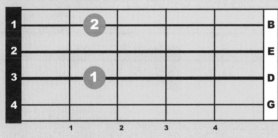

-2-	-2-	-2-	B
-0-	-0-	-3-	E
-2-	-2-	-4-	D
-0-	-4-	-0-	G

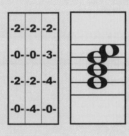

G NINTH (G9)

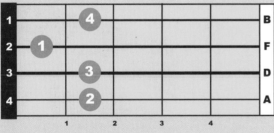

-2-	-0-	-5-	B
-2-	-1-	-5-	F
-1-	-2-	-4-	D
-2-	-4-	-0-	A

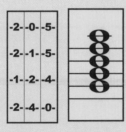

G SUSPENDED FOURTH (Gsus4)

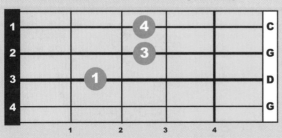

-3-	-5-	-5-	C
-3-	-3-	-8-	G
-2-	-0-	-0-	D
-0-	-0-	-0-	G

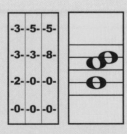

THE CHORD DICTIONARY

Chords in the Key of A♭/G♯

A♭ (G♯) MAJOR (A♭)

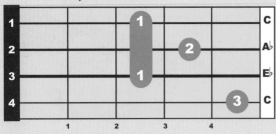

-3-	-6-	-6-	C
-4-	-4-	-4-	A♭
-3-	-0-	-8-	E♭
-5-	-8-	-5-	C

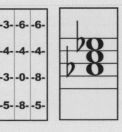

A♭ (G♯) MINOR (A♭m)

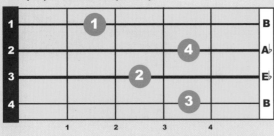

-2-	-6-	-6-	B
-4-	-4-	-7-	A♭
-3-	-3-	-8-	E♭
-4-	-4-	-8-	B

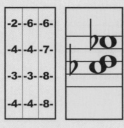

A♭ (G♯) DOMINANT SEVENTH (A♭7)

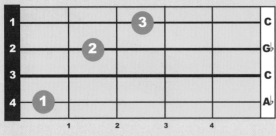

-3-	-3-	-3-	C
-2-	-2-	-4-	G♭
-0-	-3-	-6-	C
-1-	-1-	-5-	A♭

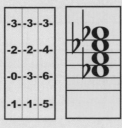

A♭ (G♯) MAJOR SEVENTH (A♭maj7 or A♭ △)

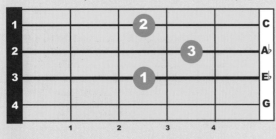

-3-	-3-	-3-	C
-4-	-3-	-4-	A♭
-3-	-3-	-7-	E♭
-0-	-1-	-5-	G

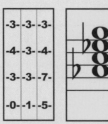

A♭ (G♯) MINOR SEVENTH (A♭m7)

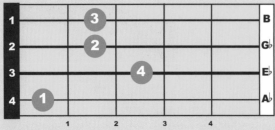

-2-	-6-	-6-	B
-2-	-4-	-7-	G♭
-3-	-6-	-6-	E♭
-1-	-4-	-8-	A♭

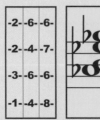

A♭ (G#) DIMINISHED (A♭ dim or A♭°)

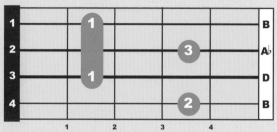

-2-	-5-	-5-
-4-	-4-	-7-
-2-	-8-	-8-
-4-	-4-	-7-

B
A♭
D
B

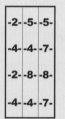  

A♭ (G#) AUGMENTED (A♭ aug or A♭+)

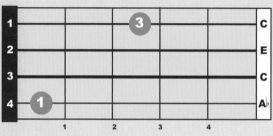

-3-	-3-	-7-
-0-	-4-	-8-
-0-	-4-	-8-
-1-	-5-	-5-

C
E
C
A♭

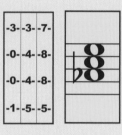 

A♭ (G#) SIXTH (A♭6)

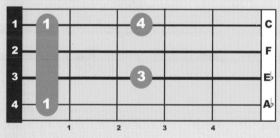

-3-	-3-	-8-
-1-	-4-	-8-
-3-	-5-	-8-
-1-	-1-	-8-

C
F
E♭
A♭

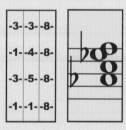 

A♭ (G#) NINTH (A♭9)

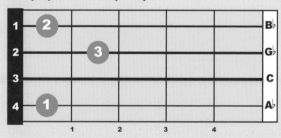

-1-	-3-	-6-
-2-	-2-	-6-
-0-	-3-	-6-
-1-	-3-	-5-

B♭
G♭
C
A♭

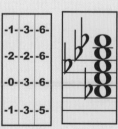 

A♭ (G#) SUSPENDED FOURTH (A♭ sus4)

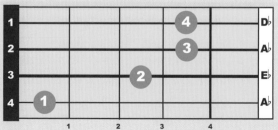

-4-	-6-	-4-
-4-	-4-	-4-
-3-	-3-	-8-
-1-	-6-	-8-

D♭
A♭
E♭
A♭

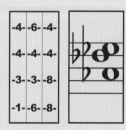 

Looking After Your Uke

The ukulele is just about the lowest-maintenance instrument imaginable. It really won't require any complex or arcane skills to keep your uke in tip-top condition. That said, if you keep a well-maintained instrument it will always sound better — and it will be nicer to play.

String Solutions

Although you do need to look after the body, neck and tuning pegs of your uke, with care the instrument's basic hardware should last for many years — if not a lifetime. The strings, however, are another matter. They will either wear out or sometimes simply snap. Before we look at how to replace them, though, let's take a more general look at the strings themselves.

String technology has come a long away in recent years. As with the acoustic guitar, ukuleles originally used cat-gut strings. (They weren't actually made from the intestines of cats but sheep, goats or cattle.) During the 1940s, nylon strings gradually became the norm; they were cheaper to produce, cost less to buy

Soprano ukulele strings

and created a more consistent sound, and are still widely used today.

Many modern players, however, favour strings made from newly developed plastics. Fluorocarbon was originally designed for use with fishing lines, but was found to produce strings that have greater strength than nylon and also generate a louder and brighter sound. A more recent proprietary material to appear is Aquila's Nylgut. Developed in Italy, this was an attempt to create a synthetic string that replicated the sound and feel of traditional gut strings. Both are now very popular choices.

TOP TIP!

Many of the cheaper ukuleles are routinely fitted with nasty, low-quality nylon strings. The simplest, cheapest and most immediately noticeable upgrade you can make is to replace them with a high-quality set from one of the more reputable string manufacturers, such as Aquila, D'Addario, Martin or Fender. The difference can be as dramatic as owning a new instrument!

Steel Strings

Whilst it is possible to fit steel strings to the most common types of ukulele – soprano, concert and tenor – it isn't necessarily advisable. Whilst some tenor players prefer a low bottom string, which is likely to be nylon with a steel winding, the tension from the top three steel strings will place pressure on the bridge and neck, and that could damage the instrument. The recommended rule of thumb is to avoid using steel strings unless you know for sure that your uke has been designed to accommodate them. And, of course, with steel strings you will lose the characteristic ukulele sound. If you do want something approaching that kind of sound, some manufacturers produce titanium strings that are less likely to cause harm to your instrument.

Removing Your Strings

At some point you will have to replace the strings on your ukulele. Removing the existing strings is a pretty simple process. Some claim that when you change a set of strings you should replace them one at a time. Although this will release tension on the neck, it will be nothing like enough to cause damage in the body or neck joint. It really is a matter of personal preference: removing all of the strings at once gives you the opportunity to give the fingerboard and frets a thorough clean; changing them one at a time makes it easier to maintain the overall tuning.

There are two ways you can remove strings. Simply detune the selected string by turning the tuning peg clockwise until the string is so loose around the capstan that it can be pulled out of the hole. At the opposite end, push the string back through the hole in the bridge and loosen the knot until it becomes untied (see bright).

The more direct approach is to take a pair of wire cutters and simply snip the string and remove the debris at either end.

WHEN TO CHANGE STRINGS

So how often do you need to restring your ukulele? Clearly you have to do it when the strings break! Otherwise it's really a matter of personal taste. Although ukulele strings are more forgiving than their guitar counterparts, over time they lose their brightness of sound. The speed at which they wear out will be largely dependent on how often you play your ukulele and the sweat in your fingers; strings may fray where they are strummed, and also begin to "notch" where they come into contact with the frets.

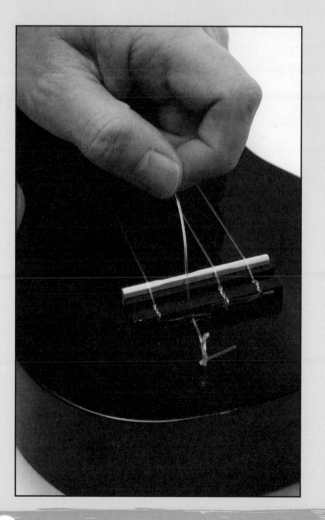

Putting on the New Strings

Restringing a ukulele can be a slightly tricky process, and if you don't get it right the strings can actually slip out of tune quite easily. Specific instructions will depend on whether your instrument is equipped with a tie-bar bridge or the less common slotted bridge.

Stringing a Tie-Bar Bridge

Found on most ukuleles, the tie-bar bridge features a channel that each string passes through and is then held in place with a knot. This can be quite a tricky process so let's go through it one step at a time.

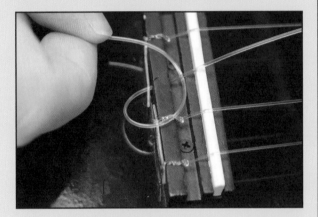

1. Take a new string and, from the headstock side of the bridge, push it through the channel until there is around 7.5cm (3 inches) of string poking out the other side. Take the short end and wrap it back over the top of the bridge and back under the string.

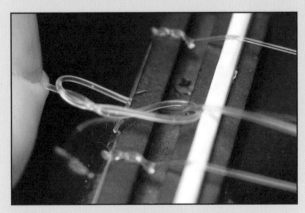

2. Take the end and push it under the loop. Thread the end through the loop and back around. Do this twice.

SLOTTED BRiDGE

If your ukulele doesn't have a tie-bar bridge it will instead have a slotted bridge. These are much simpler to restring – you simply tie a knot in one end of the string and thread it through the slot. A single knot won't do the job, though, as it can easily unravel: go for a double or figure-of-eight knot .

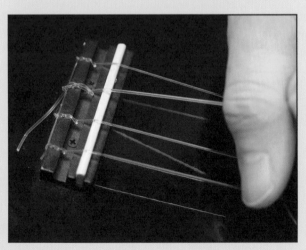

3. Hold the short end down against the bridge with one hand while pulling the other end tightly. This will lock the end of the string in place. (If the end slips through try it again – this can be pretty tricky for beginners.)

Stringing at the Tuning Peg

Once you have the string fitted at the bridge you then have to secure the string at the tuning peg. On most ukuleles, the tuning pegs are fitted to the rear of the headstock with the tuning post (the part to which the string is fitted) protruding through the top; a relatively small number of ukuleles feature a slotted headstock similar to those found on classical guitars. These are secured in a slightly different way (see page 106).

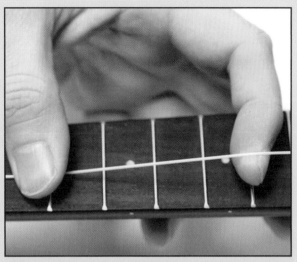

1. Before you thread the string, ensure that the open hole in the post of the tuning peg is facing the three o'clock position – approximately perpendicular to the side of the headstock. With the end of the string still held taut, thread the end through the hole from the centre of the headstock so that the end pokes out of the side.

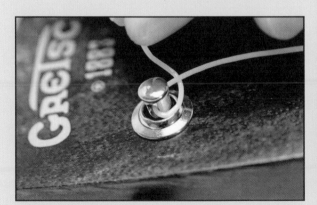

2. Bring the tip of the string around the front of the tuning post and back under the string, forming a loose knot. Bring the tip of the string around the front of the post and back under the string.

3. Keep the string taut between the bridge and the nut. Do this by holding the string down against the fingerboard and the thumb, and pushing it up with the forefinger.

4. With the string still stretched between the thumb and fingers, turn the button of the tuning peg until the string is tight. (A guitar string-winder will fit the tuning pegs of a ukulele if you happen to have one of those.)

Stringing a Slotted Headstock

If you have a ukulele with a classical-guitar-style slotted headstock you will have to adopt a slightly different threading technique.

1. Pass the end of the string over the top of the horizontal roller and poke it through the hole in the tuning post from underneath.

2. Fold back about 13cm (half an inch) of the tip of the string to create a loop and pass it over the string coming out of the other side of the roller.

3. Push the tail and the folded end down into the hole so that it traps the string in place. This can be a little tricky and might take a few attempts for you to get it right.

4. If you pull the slack the string should be held firmly in place in the roller. Finally, turn the tuning peg until the string is taut.

Stretching the Strings

Before you attempt to tune up, you should give the string a stretch, tugging it tightly somewhere over the instrument. You might be surprised at how dramatically the tension alters when you do this on new strings,

FRICTION TUNERS

Almost all modern ukuleles are fitted with metal geared tuning pegs. These usually function at a "gear ratio" of 14:1 – meaning that the tuning peg button has to be "turned 14 times for the string post to make a single revolution. This allows for very fine tuning. Very old ukuleles are fitted with friction pegs. These are immediately identifiable since the peg passes through the headstock from the back. Working in the same way as a violin, since these have no gearing mechanism they have an effective ratio of 1:1. This makes fine tuning quite tricky, especially for beginners. Frankly, as traditional as they are, these are probably best avoided!

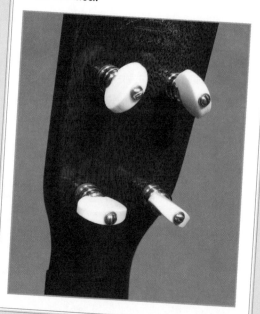

which is mainly a result of the clamping of the string at the tuning peg.

New strings need a little time to settle in, so don't be surprised to experience some temporary tuning drift when you first fit a replacement set.

Looking After Your Ukulele

If you want your ukulele to provide you with years of faithful service then you need to give it a bit of loving care when it's not being played. This certainly means giving it a quick clean after use, mainly to get rid of the corrosive effects of the sweat from your hands. Periodically you should also give it a more thorough going over.

You should also give some thought to how you store your ukulele when not in use and, if you take it out and about to play, how you protect it from dings and other damage while in transit.

Everyday Cleaning

Here's a very basic maintenance checklist that uses little more than a simple dry dust cloth; if you find light grease marks then you can dampen the edge of the cloth with a solution of lukewarm water and washing up liquid. You can buy specialised cleaning fluids for acoustic instrument bodies – anything designed for a guitar will work – but they're barely worth the money. Conditioners for the fingerboard are another matter, though (see page 108).

Although ukulele bodies come in a variety of finishes, this really won't cause any damage. Take care if you're tempted to use furniture sprays; this will be fine for bodies sealed with polyurethane varnish but really not advisable for natural wood finishes.

CLEANING FLUIDS

A naphtha solvent is really useful for all kinds of musical instrument cleaning – from the body and frets to the gears of the tuning pegs. It's especially good for getting rid of nasty, sticky gunk. A traditional musician's tip was to use lighter fluid for the same process; famous brands like Ronsonol and Zippo may no longer use naphtha in their formulation but they may still make for effective cleaning agents. (By the way, these are all perfectly safe solutions so long as you take sensible precautions like working in a ventilated space.)

1. Wipe down the body of your instrument with the dry cloth, especially the areas that have been in direct contact with your hand.

2. Wrap the cloth around the back of the neck and rub along the full length a few times. Since this will have been touching the palm of your hand it might get a bit a bit sticky, so use the cleaning solution (or naphtha if you have any to hand).

3. Now go to the headstock, wiping the front and back with the cloth, as well as all four of the tuning pegs and the buttons.

4. Carefully wipe down the strings. First run the cloth along the top of the strings and then thread the cloth under the strings so that you also clean the fingerboard (see above).

Fingerboard Care

Every so often it's a good idea to give your ukulele more thorough attention. The ideal time for this is when you change your strings as this especially gives you unimpeded access to the fingerboard and frets.

Since the fingerboard is in constant contact with the tips of your fingers it will attract all kinds of sweat and grime that can accumulate on the surface and around the frets. Since the fingerboard on many ukuleles is made from untreated hardwood like ebony or rosewood it needs to be "fed" to protect it from drying out, and you don't want that to happen as it can cause splits or cracks. You can tell when this might be happening as you'll notice patches of fading colour appearing. Lemon oil is one of the most common treatments for feeding fingerboards, and there are numerous proprietary mixtures which are generally aimed at guitarists but will work well for ukes as well. (Note: avoid lemon oils intended for general furniture use as these are likely to have unwanted additives.)

1. If your ukulele has only been used moderately and stored in case or gigbag then cleaning the fingerboard with damp paper towel might be enough – and most of us just use our own saliva for that! For slightly heavier dirt, use naphtha and leave it soak for few moments before wiping off vigorously with a cloth. One neat trick for dealing with heavier grime is to scrape using the edge of a credit card (see right); push the edge along the full width of the fingerboard from one fret to the next and then wipe off the accretion with paper towel.

2. The heaviest build-up will be around the edges of the frets. If ignored, in extreme cases, this can cause the frets to corrode. Wrap some paper towel around your thumbnail and run it along the edge of each fret. For a deeper clean, especially if the frets have been affected, is to give the whole fingerboard a clean using grade 0000 wire wool. Don't worry, this is the finest grade you can get so you won't end up filing

TRICKY SPACES

A toothbrush makes an ideal tool for getting into tricky areas like the back of the tuning pegs, or for lightly "scrubbing" the grime at the frets.

down the frets! Rub along the grain of the wood and when you've finished wipe it down with a damp paper towel.

3. When the fingerboard has been given a good clean then you can feed it with some lemon oil (or other conditioning mixture). You should certainly do this if you've used solvents like naphtha, which will have the effect of removing natural oils from the wood. Apply a few drops of the oil to a clean cloth and apply to the fingerboard. Leave it for five minutes before wiping it off with a paper towel.

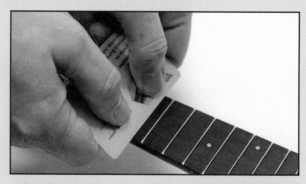

A credit card can be used to scrape grime from the fingerboard.

Lemon oil can be used to feed the natural wood in the fingerboard.

Storing your Ukulele

There's no question that the safest way of taking care of your ukulele when it's not being played is by keeping it out of harm's way in a case. Even the cases that come with the cheapest soprano ukes – which are little more than ukulele-shaped plastic bags – will offer some protection from dust, direct sunlight and minor knocks. But a far better solution is to use a dedicated "gig bag" or a hard case.

Gig Bags

Cheap and handy, gig bags are made from canvas and are sometimes padded with handles for carrying by hand or on your back. Most decent-quality models are sold with a gig bag, which will keep your ukulele reasonably well protected. They are also usually fitted with an assortment of zip-up pockets; these are useful for carrying spare strings, strap, tuner or sheet music. Don't forget, though, that ukuleles are small and delicate musical instruments, and if someone sits on your gig bag, or drops it down a flight of stairs, your uke probably won't survive!

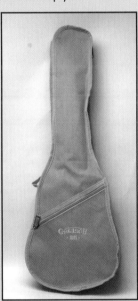

Hard Case

For maximum security, a padded hard-shell case is the answer. These can be bought for less than £50 and are a worthwhile investment if you have an expensive instrument, perform on stage or generally travel around. You can get hard cases in a box shape or the classic figure-of-eight style that traces the contour of the instrument. The downside of a hard case, though, is that it won't provide you with as much extra space for accessories.

Wall Hangers

If you like to keep your ukulele out in the open when you're at home it's best not to leave it laying around propped up against a wall or laying on an armchair – that's just asking for trouble. Ukes will sit very nicely on wall hangers designed for guitars, although you should first make sure that the headstock is sufficiently wide to fit in the slot (see right).

Violin Stand

Although dedicated ukulele stands are not very common, a uke will fit on devices designed for other small-bodied stringed instruments, such as the violin or mandolin. These are particularly good if you play on stage and can even be positioned on a wide shelf.

ENVIRONMENT

Wood is a natural material that will respond to its environment. In particular it doesn't like extremes of temperature or humidity – and shifts from one to the other even more so. This can cause the wood to dry, expand, contract, crack Leaving your ukulele in direct sunlight for long periods will cause dehydration, making the wood more brittle. If you live in an area where the air is dry, fit a cheap, miniature battery-operated humidifier in your ukulele case; if the air is damp, which may cause warping, leave a pack of silica gel in the case.

LOOKING AFTER YOUR UKE

Troubleshooting

Ukuleles are pretty low-maintenance instruments, so there are only a few things that are likely go wrong. Most of these are down to the way the ukulele is set up and can usually be fixed. It should be said, though, that with a ukulele – like most other things in life – you tend to get what you pay for, and the £15 instrument you bought online, and that goes out of tune the further you play up the fingerboard, might require more work than its worth. Let's look at some of the most annoying things that can happen.

My Ukulele Won't Stay In Tune

Keeping your ukulele in tune is a fundamental requirement. In most cases this problem should be fairly easy to remedy.

New Strings

If you've fitted new strings they need some time to settle – they simply may not have "bedded in" yet. One at a time, get each string in tune and then give it a little tug – put your thumb under the string and give it a tug. Release the string and play it again; if it's gone out of tune, retune and repeat until the string stays in tune.

Check for Slippage

If your string won't stay in tune after stretching it's likely to be a problem in the way it was tied at the bridge or, more commonly, at the tuning peg. Detune the string and remove it from the tuning peg. Put it back on carefully following the instructions on page 105.

Check the Tuning Peg

The gear wheel in the tuning peg is held in place with a small screw. If it's too tight you won't be able to turn the button; if it's too loose then it may unspool of its own accord putting the string out of tune. Take a crosshead screwdriver and apply a small amount of pressure as you turn it clockwise (see right).

INTONATION

If your ukulele gradually goes out of tune the further you play up the fingerboard then the intonation is off, which means that the bridge and saddle have not been fixed in the correct position. Unfortunately, since ukulele bridges don't allow for horizontal adjustment there isn't a lot you can do, short of removing and refitting the bridge yourself. To test out the intonation, play the 12th fret harmonic followed by the 12th fret itself. The notes should be identical. If the fretted note is flat compared to the harmonic, then the bridge needs to be moved fractionally forward. This really does come under the "expert surgery" category; if it's a problem, and your uke is a cheap, low-quality instrument, then you might be better off giving it up as a bad job and buying a new one. Otherwise, good luck!

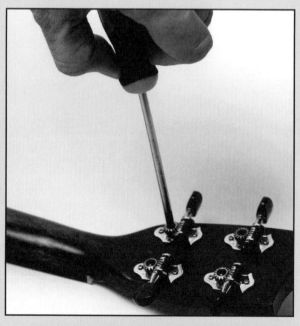

Tighten the gear wheel using a crosshead screwdriver.

The Strings are too High or Buzzing

On some low-cost ukuleles very little attention is given to setting up the "action" – the height of the strings above the frets. So how high is too high? To a degree, it's a matter of preference, although the higher the action, the harder it will be to press the strings down against the fingerboard; if it's too low then the strings may buzz against the frets. Let's look at raising and lowering the action.

Lower the Action

To reduce the height of the strings above the fingerboard you have to also reduce the height of the saddle – the white piece of plastic or bone that sits loosely in the bridge and is clamped in place by the tightened strings. Begin by slackening the strings so that you can remove the saddle. To lower the action you need to file the **bottom** of the saddle so that it sits lower on the bridge. This is really a trial and error process, so you need to take it very carefully – remember, if you file too much off the saddle you can easily end up with too low an action. A good tip here is to attach a piece of tape to mark below the area you need to remove.

1. Ideally you should do this holding the saddle in a vice so you can easily control how much you are taking off.

2. Take a fine hand file and carefully file down to the point marked by the tape. Place the saddle back onto the bridge, retune the strings and test. If the action is still too high then take a little more off the bottom of the saddle.

Raise the Action

To make the strings sit higher above the frets you have two options. You can buy a new "blank" saddle and follow the steps above to file it down to the correct height, or you can use a shim in the bridge slot. This can be any material – a piece of card, a sliver of wood – so long as it fits in the slot beneath the saddle.

FIXING THE NUT

If the string buzzing is concentrated around the first two or three frets but fine everywhere else on the fingerboard the problem may be the height at which the slots in the nut have been cut. In this case it would suggest they are too low. We have two options here: one is to remove the nut altogether and replace it with a new one; the other is to fill in the slots and recut them. Removing the nut is usually a fairly easy process – a gentle tap at the side with of the nut with a screwdriver and mallet will do the trick. You can then glue a new one in place. An old trick for filling an overcut nut is to mix baking soda with superglue, spread it carefully in the slot and recut it when dry. It's a messy process and only worth performing on a reasonable quality ukulele.

Use a fine modelling file to alter the height of the saddle.

Index